PR
MARIAN WF
LA

"I am pleased to have been selecte⸺⸺⸺⸺⸺⸺⸺⸺⸺ as
championed the rights of children in this century, as one of her mentors.
It is time for every one of us to stand up for children just as I sat down
for freedom."   —Mrs. Rosa L. Parks

"Marian Wright Edelman is *a hero* to countless young men and women, of
all colors and of all nationalities; so it is insightful to read of those who
have influenced her own life.

   In September 1967, Marian Wright visited Martin in Atlanta. She was
very persuasive and determined. We thought it was as if a whirlwind had
come through. Marian made her point and presented a plan that was
sound and succinct. These qualities would later lead her to great success
when she founded the Children's Defense Fund."   —Andrew Young

"*Lanterns* is a book to light anyone's way."   —*Essence* magazine

"Marian Wright Edelman is a *consistently illuminating and inspiring source
of wisdom* for American society. In this book we learn of the springs
from which she drank to nourish her mind, her soul and her uniquely
generous life. Take and read."

—J. Bryan Hehir, professor of the
practice in religion and society, Harvard Divinity School

"True to her untiring and relentlessly devoted spirit, [Marian Wright
Edelman] shows how mentors can shape and encourage lives."
—*Boston Globe*

LANTERNS

LANTERNS

A Memoir of Mentors

MARIAN WRIGHT EDELMAN

To Marge

*with thanks for all you
do for children. It was a
joy to have shared a meal
of children with you.*

Marian Wright Edelman

Aug 16, 2003

Perennial

An Imprint of HarperCollinsPublishers

First Perennial edition published 2000.

Designed by Anne Chalmers

Library of Congress Cataloging-in-Publication Data
Edelman, Marian Wright.
  Lanterns : a memoir of mentors / Marian Wright Edelman.
  p. cm.
  ISBN 0-06-095859-6
  1. Edelman, Marian Wright. 2. Mentoring—United States. 3. Edelman, Marian Wright—Friends and associates. 4. Afro-American women social reformers—Biography. 5. Edelman, Marian Wright—Philosophy. 6. Conduct of life. 7. Children—United States—Conduct of life. I. Title.
E185.97.E33 A3   2000
371.102'092—dc21   00-033430

00 01 02 03 04 ❖/RRD 10 9 8 7 6 5 4 3 2 1

This book is dedicated in loving gratitude
to three childhood community mentors and elders

MRS. THERESA KELLY—"MIZ TEE"

MRS. LUCY MCQUEEN—"MIZ LUCY"

and

MISS KATE WINSTON—"MIZ KATE"

to my wonderful sister, partner, and gifted teacher

OLIVE WRIGHT COVINGTON

and to the memories of our parents

ARTHUR JEROME AND MAGGIE LEOLA BOWEN WRIGHT

May their faith and family legacies bless and live on
in their children's children and in generations to come.

❧ ACKNOWLEDGMENTS ❧

Special thanks are due Manette Adams—Mrs. Harry Baker Adams—whose stewardship of my lost and forgotten Spelman College diary provided the impetus for this book. She discovered it in the Yale University chaplain's house, where I had lived for a year with the William Sloane Coffin, Jr., family; took it with her to Trumbull College; patiently deciphered my indecipherable handwriting as she prepared to move again; and kindly returned this living history of youthful struggle and engagement in the Civil Rights Movement. Its memories have nourished and reminded me of the rich texture of life shared with heroic adults and young people during the exciting civil rights years.

I am so grateful to family and friends who helped me complete this book. My son, Joshua, a public school teacher and founder and director of a youth development program which includes mentoring, read an early draft and provided wise advice.

Anne and Guido Calabresi, Laura and Dick Chasin, and Gianna Celli and her colleagues at the Rockefeller Foundation's conference center, the Villa Serbelloni, provided beautiful spaces and silence to write.

I am deeply grateful for the indispensable help of my colleagues at the Children's Defense Fund, especially Ivanna Weikert Omeechevarria, Kathy Tindell, Beth Kaufman, Paul Smith, and Janet Simons; and of Deanne Urmy, my editor and friend at Beacon Press.

And, as always, I thank my husband and partner, Peter Edelman, for patiently being there.

CONTENTS

LESSON 1: Always remember that you are God's child.
No man or woman can look down on you and
you cannot look down on any man or woman or child.

LESSON 2: Don't wait for, expect, or rely on favors.
Count on earning them by hard work and perseverance.

LESSON 3: Call things by their right names.

LESSON 4: Don't listen to naysayers offering
no solutions or take *no* or *but* for an answer.

LESSON 5: Don't be afraid to stick your neck out,
to make mistakes, or to speak up.

LESSON 6: Keep your word and your commitments.

LESSON 7: Be strategic, focus, and don't scatter your energies
on many things that don't add up to a better whole.

LESSON 8: Watch out for success.
It can be more dangerous than failure.

PREFACE

O God, I thank You for the lanterns in my life
who illumined dark and uncertain paths
calmed and stilled debilitating doubts and fears
with encouraging words, wise lessons, gentle
touches, firm nudges, and faithful actions along my
journey of life and back to You.

IT IS MY GREAT JOY to share some of the great lives and spirits of mentors who have enriched, informed, and helped shape my life. Many of them helped shape our times and national life.

I was born in the sturdy white wood parsonage at 119 Cheraw Street in Bennettsville, South Carolina, as the last of five children of Rev. Arthur Jerome and Maggie Leola Bowen Wright. My birth house is now a Children's Defense Fund office.

I have always felt blessed to be born who I was, where I was, when I was, and with the parents I had. As a Black girl child growing up in a small segregated southern town, I could never take anything for granted and never for a moment lacked a purpose worth fighting, living, and dying for, or an opportunity to make a difference if I wanted to. I was richly blessed with parents and community elders who nurtured me and other children and tried to live what they preached. They believed in God, in family, in education, and in helping others.

I did not come into or get through life alone. Neither did you. Our mothers had to push to get us here. And our fathers had to help too. My parents needed and got help in raising me and my sister and three brothers from our neighbors and friends in their church and community, some of whom you will meet here. They tried unceasingly to protect children from the unfair assaults of southern racial segregation and injustice by weaving a tight family and community fabric of love around us.

This book is not about professional or volunteer mentoring programs for children and youths or about career mentoring for those seeking to move up corporate or other professional ladders. I applaud these important efforts that help children and young adults, especially women and minority group members, get a secure foot in the job door and penetrate the invisible but often still impenetrable glass ceilings constructed by centuries of White male privilege and power. However necessary, these programs are not the answer to the daily needs all children have for consistent, caring, and responsible adults at every stage of life.

This book is about the crucial influences of the *natural daily* mentors in my life—my parents, community co-parents and elders, preachers, teachers, civic and civil rights leaders. It is about the impact of cultural, social, economic, and political forces that created the external context within which my family and Black community elders lived, and about how they influenced and shaped my perceptions and life choices. The challenge faced by Black parents when I was growing up was daunting. They had to affirm and help us children internalize our sanctity as children of God, as valued members of our family, of the Black community, of the American community, and of the entire human community, while simultaneously preparing us to understand, survive in, and challenge the prevailing values of a legally segregated nation, with a history of slavery, that did not value or affirm us as equal citizens or practice the self-evident belief that "all men are created equal" as its founding fathers professed.

Black parents—and all parents—face these same challenges today to help children define who they are and what to value in a culture that assigns worth more by extrinsic than intrinsic measures; by racial, gender, and class rather than human values; by material rather than spiritual values; by power rather than principle; by money rather than morality; by greed rather than goodness; by consumerism rather than conscience; by rugged individualism rather than community; and that glorifies violence above nonviolence.

I cannot recall a single one of the mentors I share with you in this book ever talking to me just about how to make a living or to get a job—worthy and necessary goals. They all stressed how to make a life and to find a purpose worth living for and to leave the world better than I found it. Their emphasis was on education, excellence, and service—not just on career. Their message was that if I were excellent I'd have less trouble securing a job—even as a young Black person. I can't remember the clothes a single one of them wore or the kind of car they drove or whether they drove a car at all. What I do remember is their integrity, courage in the face of adversity, perseverance, and shared passion for justice and a better life for children—their own and other people's—and for education as a means to the end of helping others. With one exception, Charles E. Merrill, Jr., son of the scion of the Merrill Lynch brokerage firm, none had much money. Some of them had none and lived hand-to-mouth by the grace of God and friends. And Charles Merrill knew that money was a means to help others and not an end. He used his to give dozens of young women and men like me and Alice Walker a chance to travel and study abroad and to experience the world he had been privileged to see.

Many of my mentors were well educated but many did not have much or any formal education. However they valued education for their children and were very astute about life. Some of the wisest words I have heard and most important lessons I have learned did not come from Harvard or Yale or Princeton or law school or Ph.D. trained mouths. They came from poor women and men educated in the school of life. Their books were struggle. Their pencils and pens were sharpened by poverty. Their mother wit was created by the daily battle for survival. Their inner faith was nourished by their outer losses. Their eyes were riveted on searching for and doing God's will rather than human ways, and their standards were divine rather than human justice.

I have always wanted to be half as good, half as brave, and half as faithful as the great women of my childhood and young adulthood like Miz Tee, Miz Lucy, Miz Kate, Mrs. Fannie Lou Hamer, and Mrs. Mae Bertha Carter, whom I introduce here. They represent countless unsung lives of grace, women who carry on day-in and day-out trying to keep their families, churches, and communities together and to instill by example the enduring values of love, hard work, discipline, and courage.

When Miss Osceola McCarthy, an elderly Mississippi woman who washed and ironed White folks' clothes all her life, gained national prominence after giving a large portion ($150,000) of her life's savings to the University of Southern Mississippi to provide scholarships for young Blacks to enter the doors that had been closed to her, many people were amazed. I was not. In less dramatic ways, I have seen many such role models who worked hard, earned more than they thought they needed to live on, and saved the rest to share with others.

I think about them when I read about young Wall Street executives complaining about the difficulties of maintaining a "decent lifestyle" on their million-dollar salaries and bonuses. I think about Mrs. Hamer and Mrs. Carter when I hear young Black, Brown, and White people whine about how hard life is. They don't know from hard as they excuse themselves from trying and decide to give up after the first, second, fifth, or tenth failure, or dissolve into despair or lash out at others when somebody hurts their feelings or insults them. Every time I am tempted (as is often) to give up or excuse myself from "doing one more thing," I think of Miz Mae Bertha or Miz Fannie Lou who until they died called up regularly to discuss how to solve some problem they could have conveniently ignored. Their examples make me stand up when I want to sit down, try one more time when I want to stop, and go out the door when I want to stay home and relax.

From the beginning, I was surrounded by strong Black female role models from my mother to Miz Tee, Miz Lucy, and Miz Kate and other community women, to Ella Baker during my college years, to the great women of Mississippi. Black women were steady anchors who helped me navigate every step of my way through childhood, college, law school, and as I tested adult professional wings. All of my mentors encouraged me by word or example to think and act outside the box and to ignore the low expectations many have for Black girls and women.

My mentors came in both genders, and in different colors, faiths, and persuasions. Three Black men, my daddy, Morehouse College president Benjamin E. Mays, and his mentee Dr. Martin Luther King, Jr., and three White men, Morehouse College board chair Charles E. Merrill, Jr., my college professor, historian Howard Zinn, and former Yale chaplain, William Sloane Coffin, Jr., played pivotal roles at key points in my life. What they all had in common was their respectful treatment of me as an important, thinking individual human being. They expressed no sense of limits on my potential or on who they thought I could become, and they engaged me as a fellow wayfarer and struggler. They saw me inside and not just outside and affirmed the strengths I had *because* I was blessed to be born a Black girl child.

All of my mentors, men and women of different faiths and colors, in their own way personified excellence and courage, shared and instilled a vision and hope of what could be, not what was, in our racially, gender, class, and caste constricted country; kept America's promise of becoming a country free of discrimination, poverty, and ignorance ever before me; put the foundations of education, discipline, hard work, and perseverance needed to help build it beneath me; and instilled a sense of the here and now and forever faithful presence of God inside me.

In the *Odyssey*, Homer used the name Mentor for an old and faithful friend of King Odysseus. The goddess Athena impersonates Mentor to inspire and impart wisdom and encouragement to prepare Odysseus' son Telemachus for his journey in search of his father, saying: "You will not lack either courage or sense in the future." Neither the king nor his son knew where their quests would lead them or what they would find.

I look back in wonder and gratitude at my rich uncharted journey from my small hometown of Bennettsville, South Carolina, to cloistered Spelman College in Atlanta, Georgia in a segregated South, through Europe and the Soviet Union for fifteen months, back to Spelman and a changing South, into the southern Civil Rights Movement, through Yale Law School and into the north of America with its subtler but persistent racial codes, to Mississippi as a civil rights lawyer, to Washington, D.C. to help prepare for Dr. Martin Luther King's

Poor People's Campaign, and around the world with my new husband, Peter Edelman, including the war zones of Vietnam with John Paul Vann after Dr. King and Robert Kennedy were assassinated. This journey brought me to the founding of the Washington Research Project (WRP), a public interest law group, and the beginning of the Children's Defense Fund into which it evolved in 1973. I am grateful beyond words for the example of the lanterns shared in this memoir whose lives I hope will illuminate my children's, your children's, and the paths of countless others coming behind.

In many ways, the labyrinth of my life is leading back to where I began and to many of the lessons learned but too easily lost in the cacophony of noise and clutter and triviality and depersonalization afflicting so much of modern American life and culture. With others, I seek to reweave the frayed remnants of family, community, and spiritual values rent asunder in the name of progress. That much racial, social, and scientific progress has taken place over my lifetime is evident. Millions of Black children and poor children of all races have moved into the American mainstream and are better off materially. But something important has been lost as we have thrown away or traded so much of our Black spiritual heritage for a false sense of economic security and inclusion. We are at risk of letting our children drown in the bathwater of American materialism, greed, and violence. We must regain our moral bearings and roots and help America recover hers before millions more children—Black, Brown, and White, poor, middle-class, and rich—self-destruct or grow up thinking life is about acquiring rather than sharing, selfishness rather than sacrifice, and material rather than spiritual wealth.

I do not seek to go back to the segregated indignities of the days before *Brown v. Board of Education* and am grateful beyond words for the Civil Rights Movement which I was blessed to witness, share in, and benefit from, as did all Americans. So few human beings have been blessed, as I have been, to experience firsthand the convergence of such great events and great leaders. The sacrifices of Montgomery, Birmingham, and Selma, Alabama, of Jackson, Mississippi and Memphis, Tennessee to tear down America's iron curtain of racial segregation must never be forgotten or repeated. We must fight with all our might the racial, religious, and gender intolerance and hate crimes resurging today in our schools, homes, and communities. Black citizens gained the right we should always have had to sit anywhere on a bus and in a restaurant, to drink colorless water without the indignity of separate Black and White fountains, to play in public playgrounds and read in public libraries, and to escape decrepit schools without books, supplies, and well-paid teachers. But as Littleton, Colorado's massacre of children by children, New York City's police brutality, and a recent Texas lynching demonstrate, skin color or "differences" defined by someone's arbitrary standards can still trigger unjust violence.

The Civil Rights Movement immeasurably lightened the physical, mental, and emotional burden of growing up Black in America. My children and yours may find it unimaginable that my generation was not able to go to the bathroom when we had to, to drink when we were thirsty, and to eat when we were hungry—natural behaviors that required unnatural thought and preparation if you were a Black child growing up in the segregated South. What Black adult today does not painfully recall holding in urine as our parents searched for a place to stop? Who in my generation was not accustomed to packing lunches to eat in the car because there was no restaurant where we could stop and be served? And who among us cannot regurgitate the feelings of rage and resentment from having to "stay in your place," watch your words, cover your back, and hide your fear, the consequences of being born Black or different from prevailing cultural standards of beauty or acceptability.

Yet as I drive past the endless clutter of fast food restaurants on our interstates and ugly sprawling city outskirts, and am glad to be able to stop and eat and go to the bathroom, I wonder whether all the hamburgers and fries and fried chicken, which I so love, are good for me, my children, or anybody's health. I worry about the loss of dinner rituals—preparing balanced meals together, setting the table, family conversation—in this era of fast foods and instant gratification. I worry about how children will learn to cook and develop good table manners and conversational skills without seeing and doing these things regularly with parents and other adults. I worry about children not feeling useful and not learning how to take care of themselves and of their families and others through regular chores. And I worry about millions of children not learning in public schools how to read and write and compute at grade level and falling behind in our knowledge-based national and global economies. Providing *all* our children—ninety percent of whom are in public schools, the crucible of our democracy—equitable and quality education is a challenge the world's super power is failing to meet today at its peril. Military readiness is hollow if our children are not school-ready. National security means nothing if a child is not safe at home and at school.

Finally, I look around with concern at the loneliness and neediness of so many children who are trying so hard to grow up and who need parents, and other caring, reliable adults to see, hear, listen to, and spend time with them in our too careless, too fast, too busy culture. So many children are killing themselves and others because they lack enough adults in their homes, schools, communities, public life, and culture to show them a different way and to reflect lives with positive purpose and integrity. Adult hypocrisy is confusing and deadening our children's spirits and minds as they struggle through an American landmine of drugs, guns, violence, and greed poised to shatter their bodies, minds, dreams, and futures.

But I look ahead with faith and determination, firmly believing we can together build newer healthier lives, strong families, strong communities, and strong children who are good human beings. This will require reshaping national priorities and reclaiming the enduring values of compassion, fairness, and opportunity that are the bedrock of the great experiment called America.

I celebrated my sixtieth birthday in 1999 (I can't believe it and don't feel it!) and am blessed with a good husband, three great adult sons, enough money, and more honors than I can pack away. And yet I feel an urgent need to throw all caution to the winds and to risk all to try to finish the quest for justice and inclusion that our founding fathers dreamed of but did not have the courage to constitutionalize and practice. Abraham Lincoln, Harriet Tubman, Sojourner Truth, Frederick Douglass, Elizabeth Cady Stanton, Eleanor Roosevelt, Benjamin Elijah Mays, Martin Luther King, Jr., Dorothy Day, Fannie Lou Hamer, Rosa Parks, Septima Clark, Ella Baker, Charles Houston, and Thurgood Marshall did their part to finish America's unfinished symphony of freedom and justice. It is now time for the next great movement, for our children. It must be led by mothers and grandmothers of all races and faiths, with youths and all others who want to show the world that America is decent enough and sensible enough and moral enough to take care of all of its children. I invite you to join me in the urgent crusade to Leave No Child Behind® so that one hundred and one thousand years from now, our children's children will call us blessed and God will say "well done," as I know God has said or will say to the lanterns I thank in this book.

LANTERNS

❧ 1 ❧

PARENTS AS MENTORS

Arthur Jerome and
Maggie Leola Bowen Wright

THE DISTINGUISHED THEOLOGIAN Howard Thurman once described an oak tree in his childhood yard with leaves that each autumn turned yellow and died, but stayed on the branches all winter. Nothing—neither wind, storm, sleet, nor snow—dislodged these dead leaves from the apparently lifeless branches. Dr. Thurman came to understand that the business of the oak tree during the long winter was to hold on to the dead leaves before turning them loose in spring so that new buds—the growing edge—could begin to unfold. At winter's end, what wind, storm, sleet, or snow could not force off passed quietly away to become the tree's nourishment.

My parents were like that oak tree. They hung onto their children until we could blossom on our own and always put our needs ahead of their own. When I think of them, I think of integrity, consistency, high expectations, family rituals and regularity, prayer, meals, chores, church activities, study, reading, service, and play. I think of common sense and sound choices, of sacrifice and bedrock faith, of their unwavering gratitude and belief in the graciousness and presence of a Creator who gave us life, and to whom Daddy entrusted us in his will. I would have been devastated if I had ever found my parents not to be who I believed them to be. They never let us down.

Breakfast was always ready when we got up, got dressed, and got ready to go to school. A hot dinner was waiting when we came home from school around four o'clock. Our parents worked hard to keep us physically and morally clean and to maintain the rituals of family life and community work.

Mama was a pillar of Shiloh Baptist Church where Daddy was pastor. She was director of the youth and senior choirs which often practiced in our home or at church, church organist, founder and head of the Mothers' Club, and fundraiser-in-chief. Mama was a natural-born organizer of people. She organized the Mothers' Club to emphasize the importance of mothers' leadership roles at home and in the community. She organized a Cradle Roll Department and many other activities for children and young people. She raised the money to help Daddy build the new church and to pay its bills with all kinds of communitywide events and contests: baby contests; Miss Universe contests; Queen for a Day contests; hilarious male-only wedding contests. The winners who raised the most money got bundles of prizes Mama extracted from local merchants and the acclaim of an always jam-packed Shiloh Baptist Church.

With her good and faithful women friends in the Mothers' Club, she prepared hundreds of Christmas bags of cheer with fruit and candy and nuts and threw a big party in the church's educational building, which we called the "hut," for all. For those who couldn't make it into the church the church went out to them. With Daddy or Mama and then alone, after we learned to drive, my siblings and I went to deliver food and coal to the poor on Christmas Day. And we were expected to visit and do errands for the poor, elderly, and sick whenever needed throughout the year.

Mama was the creative entrepreneur in the family. Daddy could not have managed without her. She always had a dime and an idea and a streak of independence that my strong father would try in vain to rein in but could always rely on. He called her "Pal."

As I grow older, I look more and more like her. My mother's strength sustains me wherever I waver in the face of tough challenges. I remember once, after I became a civil rights lawyer in Mississippi, I brought home to visit Mama a small girl who had lost her eye when marauding Mississippi Whites sprayed buckshot through the windows of her family's house. I'd been instructed by Jeannie's mother how to remove, clean, and replace her glass eye, which I felt able to do in theory. When confronted by the reality, though, I quavered. Seeing

my hesitation, my mother gently pushed me aside, and quickly removed, cleaned, and reinserted Jeannie's glass eye without missing a
beat.

I do what I do because my parents did what they did and were who
they were. I first saw God's face in the face of my parents and heard
God's voice in theirs as they cooed, read, told stories, and sang to me.
I adored Daddy's affectionate nickname for me—"Booster." I first felt
God's love in their hands and arms and feet as they held, rocked, fed,
bathed, and walked me when I was fretful or sick. I first learned God's
caring by watching them care for me and my sister and three brothers
and for others within our family and community. When Daddy's sister Ira got sick, he moved her and her five children to our hometown
of Bennettsville, South Carolina, where she later died. Daddy and
Mama helped raise Aunt Ira's five children all of whom went on to college. When Daddy's Aunts Cora and Alice got too old to live alone in
the red hills of Gaffney, South Carolina, Daddy's birthplace, they
came to Bennettsville, where my parents tended to them. When dignified old Reverend Riddick became homeless and others in the community could not care for him, my parents began the first Black home
for the aged in our town. Mama ran it after Daddy died. My brother
Julian ran it after Mama died. His daughters, Stephanie and Crystal,
have run it since he died. Many of my childhood elders have found
a caring haven in Bennettsville when they could no longer care for
themselves.

I learned to speak the truth because it was expected and enforced in
my house. I learned profanity was unacceptable after violating this te-
net on more than one occasion and having my mouth washed out
with Octagon soap. I learned to stand up when an older person entered the room and to give him or her my seat and to say please and
thank you and yes ma'am and no sir to adults. (And I want to tell
young and older people—White, Brown, and Black—not to dare call
Mrs. Rosa Parks "Rosa" or Dr. Maya Angelou "Maya" or Dr. John
Hope Franklin "John Hope" if they are not personal friends.) We need
to reinstill respect for elders at all levels of our society and elders need
to deserve it.

I learned from my parents that marriage is a struggle and a sacred partnership between two people and a covenant with God and with the children the union brings into the world. I learned that girls are as valuable as boys and that I could go around, under, and over—or knock down—the extra hurdles girls, especially Black girls, face.

◆

My parents expected their two daughters—my big sister Olive and me—to achieve and contribute as much as their three sons, Arthur, Jr., Harry, and Julian. I recall my father's palpable disappointment, as I hid behind the tall hedge watching my sister's fiancé nervously ask my father's permission for her hand in marriage, that she, only three years out of Fisk University and a teacher at Benedict College, would think of "wasting" her education and talents by marrying so young. His expectation that she would go to graduate school first to enable herself to contribute even more to others before she married stuck with me as I attempted to give back in service the interest on my own education. My sister, a gifted teacher and teacher trainer, has more than paid her interest, and Daddy would be very proud of her as our whole family is. But I never once considered marrying in my early or middle twenties; I was too busy trying to make a difference as Daddy expected.

The American society outside my home did not share my parents' egalitarian expectations. During my childhood it was the custom of many Black parents with incomes too limited to educate all their children to send their daughters to school before their sons to make their girls less vulnerable to sexual and other humiliations in the segregated South. This led to many educated women marrying less well-educated men. In my hometown, a core of the pacesetters and mentors were refined, college-educated women. But they befriended and respected their many less formally educated women friends, who often possessed enormous mother wit, integrity, love, strength of will, and spirit that no degree could confer. This book is dedicated to three of these unlettered but kind and wise souls. I always knew deep in my soul that Mrs. Fannie Lou Hamer's eloquence, intelligence, spirit, and courage, like Mayor Unita Blackwell's brilliance, unhemmed in by the King's English that I was taught to speak and write at home and in school, were as worthy as the words uttered by those with college and professional degrees. My parents and community co-parents taught me not to put on airs or to look down on others who had had less opportunity. They understood the difference between being able to test well on paper in school and to live and serve well every day.

My parents taught us to make sound choices and to focus on the truly important. My brother Harry tells about coming home from Morehouse College for Christmas and gently chastising Daddy for allowing the family car to deteriorate. He had a heavy social agenda planned and needed the car. He also noticed that Daddy's clothes were not up to their usual standards and that his shoes needed to be replaced. Harry called all these things to his attention. Daddy smiled and quietly replied: "My credit is good and I could trade in the car in the morning. I can replace my suits and I can buy new shoes, but your tuition is due in January. I cannot do both. So I have decided to tune up the car, clean the suits, and have my shoes repaired." Daddy died with holes in his shoes several years later. But he had three children who had graduated from college, my brother Harry enrolled in divinity school, my brother Julian enrolled in college and me, at fourteen years of age, dreaming about what college I'd attend.

Daddy believed in God, in serving others, and in education. He constantly tried to be and to expose us to good role models. He invited Dr. Benjamin E. Mays, Morehouse College's great scholar-president, to come speak at our church and to stay in our home. That visit prompted my brother Harry to decide to attend Morehouse. Dr. Mays promised him a job, which was provided in the Morehouse College kitchen when Harry enrolled several years later.

Daddy would pile us children into our old Dodge and drive us to hear and meet great Black achievers whenever they came near our area. I heard Mary McLeod Bethune and other inspiring speakers at Benedict College in Columbia, South Carolina—almost 100 miles away. Daddy also would drive us to Columbia to hear Dr. Mordecai Johnson, then president of Howard University, every time he came to speak—usually for several hours—at the city auditorium. I heard illustrious Black artists Roland Hayes, Dorothy Maynor, and my great namesake Marian Anderson sing at Fayetteville State College in North Carolina. I was born a few months after Marian Anderson sang before 75,000 people, including Eleanor Roosevelt, at the Lincoln Memorial, after she'd been barred from performing at Constitution Hall in Washington, D.C. by the Daughters of the American Revolution because she was Black. On a train from New Haven to New York City many years later, I saw Miss Anderson and introduced myself as her namesake. As a brash Yale law student caught up in the throes of the Civil Rights Movement, I asked her why she had sung before some segregated audiences. She graciously and patiently explained that sometimes one has to do things one does not like to do in the short term to achieve greater gains in the long term. It's a lesson that I have experienced repeatedly over the years.

The great Black poet Langston Hughes came to my hometown twice during my childhood. The first time he did not mean to come. He was traveling through South Carolina on his way to Atlanta University in Georgia and stopped at the home of a White Presbyterian minister in nearby Cheraw, South Carolina seeking a place to spend the night. The minister, no doubt terrified at the thought of putting up or being seen with a Black man in his racially segregated small town, and with no hotels or guest houses where Black folk could stay, drove to Bennettsville, asked where the Black high school was, walked Mr. Hughes into the principal's office, said Mr. Hughes needed a place to stay, and left. Mrs. Walker, the principal's wife and my English teacher, told me she wandered into her husband's office, saw this familiar-looking stranger sitting there and thought, "It can't be." He looked at her looking at him and said hello. She said, "You can't possibly be who you look like." He answered, "Try me and see." She said, "You look like Langston Hughes, but you could not be sitting here." He replied, "I am and I am going to spend the night at your house." Shocked, she asked if he would read to her class the next day. He said he couldn't but that he would come back. And he did return and read his poems to the whole school. I especially remember "Mother to Son" and "The Negro Mother."

Later, as a senior at Spelman College in 1960, I again heard this great poet who proudly reminds us of our great common Black and human heritage. That he took time to come back to Bennettsville to read to children and that a teacher made sure her students could meet him gave me a special connection to the poet I called in my college diary "marvelous . . . down to earth and unassuming"—traits my Daddy shared. I'm so proud that a Children's Defense Fund library at the former Alex Haley farm we now own bears Langston Hughes' name.

Langston Hughes' poetry and books with his wise character "Simple" and Booker T. Washington's autobiography *Up from Slavery* were in Daddy's home library. I never met Booker T. Washington, but Daddy greatly admired his teachings about self-reliance, individual initiative, community uplift, hard work, education, and service. Thanks to Daddy, I learned how Booker T. Washington and his Tuskegee colleague and scientific genius, George Washington Carver, overcame slavery, and molded Tuskegee Institute into a pathway of hope and opportunity for thousands of Black students.

I learned to love to read because my Daddy loved to read and had a study full of books he spent time with every day. On our living room mantel was a complete miniature set of Shakespeare's works. Buying books to improve our minds was an indisputably higher priority for him than buying a toy or nonessential clothing. The value of staying up to date on the latest thinking and developments in one's field was impressed upon us as we watched Daddy and Mama subscribe to theological and church music publications and buy the latest books by leading theologians and thinkers. While cleaning out our house after Mama's death, I was awed and humbled to find years of saved magazines and clippings on teen pregnancy, family values, and race relations. Among a pile of old issues of *Christian Century* on the freezer on our enclosed back porch was one opened to a page with a quotation by Dwight David Eisenhower underlined in red: "Every gun that is made, every warship launched, every rocket fired, signifies, in the final sense, a theft from those who hunger and are not fed, those who are cold and are not clothed. This world in arms is not spending money alone. It is spending the sweat of its laborers, the genius of its scientists, the hopes of its children." I had discovered this quotation independently in a Washington, D.C. library several years before, made it into a Children's Defense Fund poster, and used it in many speeches. How reassuring yet eerie to feel Daddy's guiding hand affirming my work for children and my struggle with still misguided national priorities so many years later. Eisenhower's warning is more relevant today than ever.

Daddy and Mama did not confine their self-improvement to reading. They went to Union Theological Seminary (Daddy admired Dr. Harry Emerson Fosdick, esteemed pastor of Riverside Church, very much), to a Black Mountain, North Carolina conference center where they met E. Stanley Jones, and to Oberlin College for summer courses and other enrichment. They went away every year for a week to the Minister's Institute at Hampton Institute in Virginia, sometimes taking me along. I would wander along Hampton's waterfront and through the chapel and library at the college Booker T. Washington attended and where he later taught while my parents listened to the latest developments in their fields. I'd join them in the evenings to listen to great sermons and choirs.

My belief that I and others could do more than complain, wring hands, or give in to despair at the wrongs rife in the world stems from my parents' examples. Daddy, a teacher-preacher who never raised his voice in the pulpit and who tried to educate our congregation's mind as well as touch its heart, taught that faith required action and that action could be sustained only by faith in the face of daily discouragement and injustice in our segregated southern society. Because the public playgrounds and many public services were closed to Black children, Mama and Daddy made our church a hub for children. Boy and Girl Scout troops, boxing, skating, ball games, and other physical activities provided outlets for pent-up boys' and girls' energy. Choirs, children's days, pageants, and vacation Bible school made church a welcoming haven rather than a boring chore. And the great preachers and role models invited to speak at Shiloh helped challenge our minds and widen our horizons and remind us of the sky above and of the rainbows in the clouds.

My outrage about children who die needlessly from preventable diseases and curable sickness today is a result of my parents' sadness over the senseless death of little Johnny Harrington, who lived three doors down from our church parsonage and did not get a tetanus shot after stepping on a nail. His good and hard-working grandmother didn't have the money or the knowledge to take him to the emergency room and nobody acted until it was too late.

My concern for safe places for children to play and swim comes from the lack of public playgrounds for Black children when I was growing up and our exclusion from the swimming pool near my home where I could see and hear White children splashing happily. A childhood friend died when he jumped off the bridge into the shallow hospital-sewage-infected waters of Crooked Creek near my home and broke his neck. And I almost drowned in a segregated public lake in Cheraw, South Carolina that lacked adequate lifeguard surveillance. Daddy and Mama built a playground behind our church with a skating rink and swings and sliding boards and lights so children could play at night and Mama opened a canteen with sodas and snacks so that young people could have someplace safe and fun to go.

My advocacy for equitable health care for all and outrage that our rich nation denies it to millions comes from the horror Daddy and I felt when we witnessed a White ambulance driver arrive on the scene of a middle-of-the-night collision near our home only to drive away, leaving behind seriously injured Black migrant workers after he saw that the White truck driver with whom they had collided was unhurt.

Daddy died on May 6, 1954—eleven days before the U.S. Supreme Court's *Brown v. Board of Education* decision that he had waited and watched for. My mother carried on our family's rituals and responsibilities valiantly—doing what she had to do to continue preparing us for life.

My concern for children without homes and parents unable to care for them comes from the foster children my mother took into our home after Daddy died. I am still ashamed of my resentment and jealousy when I was asked to share my room with a homeless child for a few days. As I grew older, nearly a dozen foster sisters and brothers were reared by my mother.

An elderly White man asked me what I did for a living when I was home for my mother's funeral in 1984. I realized and told him I do, perhaps on a larger scale, exactly what my parents did: serve and advocate for children and the poor.

COMMUNITY ELDERS AS CO-PARENTS AND MENTORS

Miz Tee, Miz Lucy, Miz Kate, and Miz Amie

I LOVED IT when my parents left town to attend a convention, visit a relative, or pursue continuing education because I would get a chance to stay with Miz Tee Kelly or Miz Lucy McQueen which I loved. They were among my many kind Black community co-parents and elders who spent time with and paid attention to me. They had no children of their own but mothered many children as if we belonged to them.

Miz Tee—Mrs. Theresa Kelly—lived in a four-room unpainted house with a big front porch and a small back porch on Amelia Street in Bennettsville. Every inch of it was sparkling clean. Every Sunday night my family enjoyed Miz Tee's scrumptious dinners of fried or smothered chicken, macaroni and cheese, rice or mashed potatoes with gravy to die for, greens—collards, turnips, cabbage, or kale—and the thickest but lightest buttermilk biscuits, the recipe for which she took to heaven with her, that would melt in your mouth. Topped off by the best sweet potato pone I've ever tasted, and fresh churned ice cream, Miz Tee's dinners were a treasured Wright family ritual each Sabbath evening.

Miz Tee, when she kept me, would let me share her daily chores of ironing, cooking, washing, hanging out the clothes, and cleaning the house. She was not only a perfect housekeeper and cook, but she starched and ironed white dress shirts without a wrinkle for White folks with the heavy cast irons she hooked onto and heated around her coal-burning potbellied stove. In the room where I slept—which doubled as her living room—there was a big framed picture of Jesus walking on the water towards the boat of his terrified disciples who were afraid of capsizing in the tossing waves.

I never met anyone else in her family; I felt my family was her family. She lived alone for as long as I remember. As far as I know, she had very little formal education, but she knew her Bible and attended Sunday school and church every Sunday faithfully. She was so proud and encouraging when my sister Olive, my brothers, and I went off to college. She would send us shoeboxes filled with greasy dollar bills and fried chicken and biscuits that everyone on my dorm floor looked forward to with great anticipation. "When is Miz Tee going to send another box?" was a common question.

Miz Tee believed that God controlled everything including the length of life. When fierce lightning and thunder storms would come during summer months, Mama didn't seem so sure. She would gather all of us together, cut off the electric lights, and sit with us in the dark on the stairs in our new parsonage until the storm passed over. She was afraid of lightning strikes. One day when a big summer storm was whipping up, Miz Tee told me to go out on the back porch and bring in the clothes hanging there so they wouldn't get drenched. As I went to obey, a clap of thunder boomed and I ran back and told Miz Tee I was scared of being struck by lightning. She calmly replied, as she returned with me to the back porch to gather in the clothes, "When it's your time, it's your time, when it's not, it's not. Lightning not going to hit you less God's ready for you."

On some nights other than Sundays, my family and I visited with and ate at one or another parishioner's house, all of whom vied to outdo the other in providing hospitality for our family. As the last, and for six years, only child at home, I often accompanied my mother to her circles, Mothers' Club, and missionary society meetings. The church circles, groups of about thirty women who met regularly, were named after the great mother figures and backbones of the church—Mrs. Mary Jane Bradford, Mrs. Nanny Edwards, Mrs. Della Harrington, and Mrs. Viola Reese. So I overheard the womenfolks' talk and gossip all the time as we shared meals and engaged in various church and community chores and activities.

Because there were no washing machines or dryers, Black women in Bennettsville washed their families' clothes and White people's clothes in big washtubs, with scrubboards, soaked them in Rinso, washed out heavy stains with lye, hung them on clotheslines to dry, and ironed them with irons heated on wood- and coal-burning stoves. Sometimes Black women of our community would gather to wash clothes together at one another's houses. When they came to our yard, I helped out by hanging up the well-rinsed wet clothes on lines, taking them down after they dried, and folding them. Quiet guerrilla messages about race relations accompanied these clotheswashing exercises. Black women were ambivalent about having to wash White people's clothes, cook their food, clean their houses, and tend their children—often while leaving their own children—to make ends meet. While they were grateful for the chance to work, they did not like it that the door of opportunity was closed to them on most non-domestic jobs except teaching which required more education than most of them had received in their segregated and unequal public schools.

Unlike ours, many of the houses where Black people lived had no electricity. Miz Tee's house did not so we ate and conversed there by the soft warm light of wick-lit oil lamps. I keep one on the third floor of my home today to remember how it felt.

Every summer after the vegetable gardens and peach trees ripened, a group of women would come to our parsonage and we'd all spend days peeling peaches and apples and tomatoes, shelling peas and butterbeans, shucking corn, and cooking and canning them and making jelly for winter. And every year there was a hog-killing time. My Daddy raised chickens and hogs and kept our smokehouse filled with bacon and hams and pork chops that lasted all winter long. I don't touch a chitterling to this day—indeed flee the room at the whiff of chitterling smell—after getting sick and gagging for hours after over-indulging in a feast of them, perhaps not as thoroughly cleaned as

needed. But the communal preparation of food, the washing of chit-
terlings in tubs and hanging them on the clotheslines or fences, the
preparation of sausage and the cutting of pork chops, hams, and
bacon, the salting of meats—and sharing a portion of it with those
less fortunate—are childhood memories I'll never erase.

◆

My parents did not have to raise me and my sister and brothers alone.
The whole community helped them and me just as they helped other
people raise their children. Every place I went, there were eyes watching me and people reporting on me when I strayed into places or company or engaged in behavior they knew or thought my parents would
not approve. There was always a place other than Miz Tee's if my parents were away. Miz Lucy McQueen, a beautiful, kindly, gray-haired
church woman who taught Sunday school, would spoil me with lem-
onade and biscuits and good stew beef and did not make me eat vegetables I did not like when I stayed in her welcoming but decrepit old
house. I don't remember much of what it looked like inside, but I do
remember what it felt like: warm and loving. And I can smell the big
gardenia bushes that bloomed profusely alongside the rose bushes in
her yard. Their fragrance, and the perfect white petals that browned at
my touch, are among the sweet smells of childhood memory. I've not
had luck keeping gardenias alive for long stints in my kitchen and yard
but I'll keep trying. (My mother's hardy snake plants, though, have
nearly taken over my sunny kitchen windows.)

Miz Kate Winston is another precious elder from childhood. She
came from Washington, D.C. with a White family in the summers and
attended our church when she was in Bennettsville. I visited her once
in her home on Rhode Island Avenue in the nation's capital and waited
eagerly for her trips home when she would bring me the prettiest
dresses—different from any you could find in Bennettsville—and
more extravagant than my parents could afford or would buy.

Sometimes I stayed with Mrs. Nancy Reese, who was married to Mr.
Pierce, a master bricklayer who helped build our church and some of
the leading White homes in our town. Miz Nancy organized and led
the gleaners who went behind the senior ushers who take up the

church offerings, collecting small leftover donations in little tin containers for mission work which we counted with her after church. I loved being a gleaner and going up and down the church aisles every Sunday with Miz Nancy's other child charges.

Just as my parents did not have to raise me alone, my husband and I have been blessed with Mrs. Amie Byers to help raise our three sons. My mother sent Miz Amie to live with us and help care for our children when our oldest son Joshua was fifteen months old and our second son Jonah was an infant. She stayed for fourteen years until our third son Ezra was nine years old, treating our three sons as her own. She not only watched over them and their playmates but all the children on our Newton, Massachusetts and later Washington, D.C. neighborhood streets. A woman without a great deal of formal education, she is as smart as a whip, full of mother wit, able to fix anything, piece together any puzzle, and puzzle over any problem that arises until she solves it. Fearless with the hoe, she would chop in two the snakes I feared that plagued our country yard in upstate Chatham, New York. Full of quiet dignity, she transmitted an example of patience and calm—qualities that frayed dual-career parents often lack. My sons honor her now like a grandmother.

She never missed a graduation as our sons—she called them "my boys"—went through elementary and high school, and she celebrated their academic honors and sports achievements as we did. Although her disabled hip kept her from traveling to Stanford when Josh got his Masters and to Oxford when Jonah got his Doctorate, she was with us in spirit and sat proudly at Josh's, Jonah's, and Ezra's college commencements. I could not have made it without her. I hope my children carry deep in the recesses of their minds and spirits her constant humming of hymns and spontaneous prayers and stories of times past in Bennettsville. Her care for me and our family has carried into the present the legacy of mothering from the good women of Bennettsville for which I'm so profoundly grateful.

My having been blessed with many positive adult community mentors does not mean I don't remember, as all children do with great clarity, the times when the spoken and lived messages I received from adults diverged. A kind family friend who ran a play school for children once took me with her to visit her sister in another South Carolina town for a week. At the Greyhound Bus ticket counter, the clerk asked how old I was. Wanting to pay the cheaper child's fare, my adult friend told the ticket man I was younger than I was. I piped up and said, "No I'm not, I'm twelve." She paid the adult fare, but not so happily. I remember sensing I had done wrong by telling the truth.

We adults, myself included, often engage in small "stories" or "white lies" to cut seemingly small corners. But it is so important to try to tell the truth before children in small and big things. And when we misstate something, have a momentary lapse in judgment, or make a mistake, to admit it. Children pick up our signals and are confused when we say one thing and do another. This small incident nearly fifty years ago makes me insist on paying the right prices or fares, correct a clerk when he or she undercharges as well as overcharges me, and never return a garment I've worn but just don't like. One of my proudest moments as a parent came when I received a letter in the mail from a man who lived two streets over from our house in Washington. Two of my sons had slid and hit his parked car during a snowstorm and left a small dent in it. They did not know whose car it was so they left a note behind the windshield wiper telling the owner what had happened and where a bill for any repair could be sent. The bill arrived with the owner's note that said this was the first time an anonymous driver who had damaged his parked car had done what my sons had done. Never have I enjoyed paying a bill more, and I thought how proud my Daddy would be of his grandsons' integrity. I kept the man's letter on the refrigerator for many months.

◆

Although Miz Tee, Miz Lucy, and Miz Kate stand out most fondly in my store of childhood memories, there was a plentiful presence of adults who guided and helped us children in Sunday school, vacation Bible school, and other church activities, and in my Brownie and Girl Scout troops (my Scout leader, Miss Johnson, was also my seventh grade teacher). Mrs. Alice Thomas, the mother of my best friend, Ruth, welcomed me into her home as another family member. I would regularly visit Miss Flora Fields, whose nickname was "Scrappy" and who lovingly cared for her retarded brother, Henry, just to talk. In the summer, she and I would pick vegetables from her garden for me to take home to Mama. Black adults always waved and spoke to children. They stopped us on the streets to ask how we and our families were doing; they watched from and called me up to their porches for friendly chats; and I ran their errands. They provided buffers of love and encouragement that helped combat the negative influences of segregated small-town southern life. They helped keep the outside messages from Whites that I, a Black child, was inferior from being internalized.

Black adults did not merely tell us what to do, they engaged us in doing real work with them. My brothers worked side by side with master masons, hauling bricks and mixing cement as Daddy struggled to complete Shiloh Baptist Church, still stately today, patterned after the chapel at Benedict College. Through daily family meals, we learned how to set the table, prepare food, hold a conversation, sit up straight, say please and thank you, and thank God for the food we were fortunate to have to nourish our bodies. All my young life Daddy kept in the middle of the bulletin board of our church vestibule a newspaper cartoon of a group of affluent White people sitting at a table filled with food. All around them stood hordes of emaciated, hungry Brown people gazing at them as they ate. The caption of the searing cartoon was: "Shall we say grace?" We learned to share, to clean up after ourselves, and to take responsibility for our household's and church's yard upkeep. Regular chores at regular times were assigned and supervised.

We learned how to set priorities. Homework and housework before play. Chores before naps and movies. Running an errand or doing a deed for a needy neighbor before Saturday fun or visits with a friend. And Sunday was always about worship and fellowship and hospitality in our home and others and for visiting the sick.

The ten beautiful women in one photograph I've included in this book personify the formidable and loving network of community support with which I and many children of my generation were blessed. Four of these women were college-educated teachers married to the deacons and trustees of our church who were also our dentist, undertaker, and skilled artisans. Six of them had little or no formal education but were as smart, wise, and faithful as their more middle-class peers who lived in well-appointed homes. All were equally valued and valuable as they—together with our teachers and parents—wove a seamless safety net of caring for children. Some like Miz Prudence and Miz Glenn and Miz Rosa McCollum—who married three brothers—reflected and reinforced the importance of high academic standards as did Daddy and Mama. While stressing the importance of education, of proper English, and of reading, not a single one of them ever equated book smarts with common sense or goodness. All sought a better standard of living for all in our community but none saw money or things as the primary aim in life. Education, like money, was another means to help improve the lives of others.

Miz Tee Kelly and Miz Lucy are not home anymore to keep many of today's children when parents have to go away or are working. There aren't enough strong McCollum women left who spend as much time working with children to set high standards and to make clear their belief that every child can achieve at high levels. Too many of our churches are no longer the activity hubs and safe havens they used to be for children in strong and in struggling families. And while many Black families are better off economically today, thanks to better jobs and education and choices about where to live, too many still are not: There are still millions of poor and struggling parents whose children are falling behind in public schools that don't serve them well. And too many Black middle-class parents don't emphasize achievement and service strongly enough or exude the spiritual commitment needed to nurture the next generation of leaders that was so evident in my day. This is also true in the White and privileged community where children's needs often take a backseat to adult needs and desires.

I do not seek to reinvent the past or think we can stop the bulldozer of "progress" ushered in by technology and by the globalization of our economy. I do think, though, that we must stop and assess what we have gained and what we have lost over the past half century, and how we might adjust our institutions to meet changing child and family needs in a positive rather than in a punitive or impersonal way. The prison complex in my home county is bigger than the consolidated county high school. It costs far more to keep a prisoner who dropped out of school than to educate a child for success. With so many working families, and so many families headed by teens and single parents, and with low wages that keep millions of working families still poor, so many children are beginning school not ready to learn, and large numbers in my county, in South Carolina, and in every state in our country are going through the motions of school unable to read, write, or do math at grade level. Today some youths are committing crimes and scrawling nihilistic graffiti on the walls of my little hometown's grocery stores and waiting idly for the drug dealers' drop just like children are in many suburban or urban areas. Michael Jordan's father's body was found in my home county, slain by youthful murderers.

While there are these and other disheartening signs of trouble there are also hopeful ones. In the still sturdy clapboard house at 119 Cheraw Street where I was born and raised, the Children's Defense Fund office is headed by my sister Olive Wright Covington, a gifted educator who is working harder in "retirement" than ever before in her life. Inside, every room is teeming with activities and full of books. It is the incubator and curriculum development laboratory for Children's Defense Fund–sponsored Freedom Schools—academic, nutritional, and cultural enrichment programs that operate in my home county and in over forty other sites in rural and urban areas across America. Black college students, after training, have taught reading to and instilled a love of learning in over 12,000 five- to sixteen-year-old children in the summer and, in some communities, after school and on Saturdays. Children learn to play chess and to resolve conflicts without violence. So do their parents and college-age mentor-teachers, who stayed in school, went on to college, and have come back to reach out to teach younger children. Miz Tee, Miz Lucy, and Miz Kate would have recognized and been proud of this newest generation of mentors and young servant leaders who give children hope that they can follow positive paths to college and jobs rather than negative ones to drugs and jail.

The ultimate mission of Freedom Schools is to reengage the whole community in the lives of its children and to reweave the kind of community caring Miz Tee and others provided for my generation of children who faced a hostile segregated world. All children need adults who believe in them and expect them to achieve, who love them, and whom they love so much they live up to their expectations of success.

❧ 3 ❧
TEACHERS AND
THEIR MESSAGES

I WAS FOURTEEN years old when the landmark *Brown v. Board of Education* case was decided by the United States Supreme Court. It had a profound psychological although not immediately practical effect on me. Daddy and I had talked about the case often. His death came right before the ruling and the South's subsequent resistance to its implementation. I graduated from an all-Black high school two years later in June 1956.

It was a new school on the outside. My school district, like many throughout the South, had made a hasty effort to equalize physical facilities in order to circumvent *Brown*. But the hand-me-down books and equipment from White schools remained. The presence of Black teachers who cared about us and who often were better qualified than their White counterparts because they had fewer professional choices was a plus.

However, the racial tightrope my public school principal and teachers walked, trying hard not to rock the segregationists' boat or to jeopardize their jobs, was not lost on me or, I'm sure, on other Black children. They were content to timidly request incremental resources to help equalize educational offerings for Black children but unwilling to push hard or publicly for what was just. Like many White southerners, many Black southerners were threatened by the changes *Brown* portended. Some Black teachers feared competing with White teachers who were often better trained as a result of the unequal and segregated elementary, secondary, and higher education systems.

I cannot recall a single Black teacher in my hometown ever speaking up or organizing publicly to challenge the educational or racial status quo. Septima Clark, one of my role models whose courageous voice I describe later in this book, said the greatest disappointment in her life was the failure of her Black teacher colleagues to support the NAACP and her in the successful effort to equalize Black and White teacher pay in South Carolina—a stand for which she got fired and from which they benefited.

While most of our teachers did not stand up for children in the White world where they felt disempowered and on which they depended, many of them tried to compensate by giving each Black child personal attention. They helped ground us in our history and culture through daily singing of the Negro National Anthem by James Weldon Johnson and his brother Rosamond, "Lift Every Voice and Sing;" by holding oratorical contests in which we memorized and recited before our class (the winners recited before the whole school community) speeches by great Black historical figures; and by bringing Black speakers like Langston Hughes and other achievers to inspire us and to let us know we could go higher. They expected us to achieve and we did. Some served as our Sunday school teachers and were in and out of our homes on a regular basis. Today many teachers do not know the parents of the children they teach, visit their homes, or even live in the school district.

Teachers—like parents—make a big impression on children for good or ill. I remember as if it were yesterday how I felt when I went with one of my teachers and a church member into Belk's Department Store on Main Street when I was six or seven years old. I was thirsty and went instinctively to drink from the nearby water fountain. I recall my teacher jerking me away in panic from the "White" water fountain, water trailing down my pinafore. It was the first thing I remembered when my sister told me that she had died in her nineties. All of her many kindnesses to me and my family never erased that moment that defined her as an adult unable or unwilling to affirm my personhood and child's fragile self-image. Perhaps if she had exuded less fear or had stopped and gently explained to me that segregated water was a stupid symbol of a stupid unjust system that had nothing to do with my intrinsic worth or hers, and that she was sorry she could not do anything about it just then but that it was wrong, I might have felt differently about her then and remember her differently now. I took my tiny wounded soul home to recount my hurt to my parents and sought reassurance that I was indeed as good as White people and that it was an inferior system and not an inferior me that denied me— a thirsty, small child—water. "Whosoever gives even a cup of cold water to one of these little ones in the name of a disciple—truly I tell you, none of these will lose their reward," I had learned in Sunday school and church. I believed it and wanted adults I cared about to do so too.

I worry all the time about disappointing and letting my own children or any child down. Children look to important adults in their lives for signals about what is right and wrong, and how to interpret people or events that insult and assault their self-image. While parents and teachers cannot control or shut out so much of the vulgarity and violence bombarding our children, it is crucial that we try to listen to and talk to them about it, help them put it into a larger context, assert our values, and say what we think about it.

Like parenting, teaching is a mission, not just a task or a job. I don't care how fancy the school, how low the student–teacher ratio (which I believe should be lower), how high the pay (which I think should be higher): If children don't feel respected by adults who respect themselves, and don't feel valued for themselves and if the lotteries of their births dictate the inputs and often the outcomes of their lives, then they and all of us lose. How sad and unfair that the children who come into the world with the least—whose parents are the least able to provide them with health care, good nutrition, shelter, and stimulation—are also the children who are least likely to have access to quality developmental early childhood education. Children who are the least likely to be read to and sung to at home by their mothers, or by their fathers, whom some too seldom see or know, are the most likely to attend schools with the least qualified teachers, the poorest equipment and supplies, and the fewest counselors. They are least likely to have access to school nurses and art and music programs and computers and to have opportunities for after-school and summer enrichment programs that affluent parents can pay for. And they are likely to live in neighborhoods with fewer safe playgrounds and greater violence and drug trafficking.

These wounded child victims of violence and neglect inside and outside their homes, inside and outside their schools, are wrongly labeled as "superpredators" by some political demagogues before they are even born or can toddle. And they are unjustly portrayed in the media without individuation, analysis, or understanding as an undifferentiated group of young irredeemable criminals who ought to be jailed with adults. The last thing any young offender needs is adult criminal mentors.

Some professors and students at predominantly White schools and universities also engage in unjust stereotyping and place the burden on all minority students to prove they are not less able than all White students. Minority students are often so wounded by the time they reach college campuses that they need to be prepared with the tools of self-understanding and combat needed to fight their battles to achieve in society just as my generation was prepared to fight these same battles.

But stereotyping, hate crimes, and intolerance are not limited to attacks on Black youths. The Littleton, Colorado school massacre with its Nazi overtones, religious intolerance, and violent punishment of those who rejected or annoyed the privileged perpetrators is a loud alarm bell for teachers—and all adults—to clarify, live, and inculcate more positive values and to build more positive learning communities for our young.

SPELMAN COLLEGE— A SAFE HAVEN

Benjamin Elijah Mays, Howard Zinn,
and Charles E. Merrill, Jr.

I DID NOT WANT to go to the all-Black, all-women Spelman College in Atlanta, Georgia, with its reputation as a tea-pouring very strict school designed to turn Black girls into refined ladies and teachers. I desperately wanted to attend all-Black Fisk University from which my sister Olive had graduated. It had a distinguished history with alumni like Dr. John Hope Franklin, Dr. W. E. B. DuBois, civil rights attorney Constance Baker Motley, and professors like Arna Bontemps, Langston Hughes' great friend and collaborator, artist Aaron Douglas, and the world-renowned Fisk Jubilee Singers. Fisk also held the lure of my possibly snagging a Black doctor husband from nearby Meharry Medical College which I considered a better catch than a mere graduate of Morehouse, the all-Black men's college across the street from Spelman from which Dr. King and many stellar Black male leaders graduated.

But after a family debate about whether I should go to a "White" university in the immediate aftermath of *Brown v. Board of Education*, which we hoped would usher in a new America, and under maternal duress, I did enroll at Spelman. The college's generous scholarship offer and the presence of my Daddy's best friend, Morehouse religion professor and pastor of Providence Baptist Church, Lucius Tobin, a brilliant but depressive man, tipped the scales and landed me on the train to Atlanta. That my much loved big brother Harry, my surrogate father after Daddy died, had graduated from Morehouse (so did his son, Harry, Jr., many years later), was a final factor in my family's deciding on Spelman.

I rebelled during the first semester of my freshman year against Spelman's rigid routines which included compulsory daily 8:00 A.M. chapel, 5:00 P.M. curfews, and dress requirements when off campus.

Spelman students were required to sign in and out, leave campus in groups of threes, and fit our romantic pursuits into a one-hour calling hour when Morehouse men could come courting in full view of stern matrons. We had fifteen minutes to get into our dormitory after dances on Spelman's campus and thirty minutes after Morehouse campus dances. Designated and well-lit routes were monitored by hawk-eyed chaperones to prevent us from straying from the straight and narrow path of propriety. In the face of so much regimentation, I would occasionally feel the need to sneak off campus to go to the movies or to Paschal's restaurant for its addictively good fried chicken.

Spelman's adults seemed to have as many eyes to watch over its students as did my home community. I got caught off campus one day and was campus-bound for three weeks by the very stern, no-nonsense, tough-love dean of students Eugenia Dunn who looked straight at and through me and said ten words as she grounded me: "From her to whom much is given, much is expected." I got the message and tried to live up to her and my parents' expectations from then on.

As a Spelman freshman, I thought I wanted to be a doctor until I met the frogs in my biology laboratory whose sustained company I contemplated without an iota of enthusiasm. I began my sophomore year trying to please my mother by becoming a music major but a Merrill Study Travel Fellowship to spend my junior year abroad changed my course and subverted my mother's desires to have at least one daughter follow in her musical footsteps.

I've never regretted, though, my years of compulsory musical training. The piano lessons my mother insisted my sister and I take, the choirs she led in which we sang, the songs we practiced in our home, the Spelman Glee Club that Dr. Willis Lawrence James directed, and the Morehouse College Sunday morning chapel choir led by the late, great Wendell Whalum, have remained indispensable sources of meditative and spiritual strength throughout my life. Music connects me to my past and was the glue of the Civil Rights Movement, holding Black communities together and renewing our spirits with the fuel we needed to struggle each day. It was the outlet for our fears and our hopes, and our language to communicate with God and each other when words failed to capture our emotions as they so often did. When the music died, the movement died. When the music dies within me now, when I am too dry to sing or play a hymn, I know I am out of balance and in emotional trouble. Like the mountains and the rhythmic ocean tides, music renews and reconnects me with life and inner spirit and the cloud of witnesses who went on before who shared the human quest for freedom and justice and for God. Music, like kindness, is a universal language that transcends race and place and connects freedom fighters and freedom seekers in Georgia, Mississippi, South Africa, and Eastern Europe. "We Shall Overcome," the anthem of the Civil Rights Movement, expresses a longing throughout the world for life beyond the now, for a life that can and will be. My husband and I were thrilled on a honeymoon stop in Prague a few days before the 1968 Soviet invasion to join with Czech citizens singing "We Shall Overcome" in one of the old town squares.

I am so glad I went to Spelman. As an all-Black women's college it gave me the latitude and safe space—one not defined by male or White folks' expectations, habits of competition, or by the need to preen and prove myself to anyone beyond myself and God—to dream my dreams and to find and forge my own path.

While I hated and hate forced segregation or forced anything, I now recognize that Spelman provided the incubation I needed after leaving home to stand on my feet confidently with anyone anywhere. The cloistered shared community and rituals prepared Spelman women to do battle outside its gates. The words of chapel speakers like Dr. Howard Thurman and Dr. Benjamin Mays worked themselves into the hidden recesses of my mind and heart and well up when needed. The exposure to past and present struggles for social justice undergirded our academic studies. And the regular interaction with our college presidents and teachers and community leaders all helped shape the adult I became.

Young people today need the same nurturance and guidance and engagement with adults that I received. They need a sense of shared purpose that comes from shared actions and struggles. And they need exposure to a wide variety of people doing worthwhile rather than frivolous or self-seeking things. I was massaged and renewed by the rich touches and words and spirits of Black womenfolk during my childhood, and I learned during my college years that there was a big wide world with all kinds of people in it and that I could stand tall amongst them.

DR. BENJAMIN ELIJAH MAYS

One of the most important people to me during my college years was Dr. Benjamin Elijah Mays, president of Morehouse College between 1940 and 1967. I first met him in 1953 when I was thirteen years old and he came to stay at my house. Daddy had invited him to speak at our church. Because there were no hotels where Black visitors could stay in my southern town (or, as Langston Hughes had learned, in any neighboring town), the pastor and parishioners always provided hospitality to strangers great and humble.

I heard and saw Dr. Mays and his beautiful wife Sadie often at Spelman or on Morehouse's campus. Students were regularly invited to their house and I was one of eight very lucky Spelman students privileged to sing with eight Morehouse students at Morehouse's Sunday morning chapel services in Sale Hall. The choir was conducted by the gifted young Wendell Whalum who made our songs and spirits soar.

I heard Dr. Mays as well as an array of other speakers from Morehouse and the outside world every week. With Spelman's 3:00 P.M. compulsory Sunday chapel coming after Morehouse's 9:00 A.M. services and Spelman's daily 8:00 A.M. chapel, my spiritual and civic education rivaled, indeed exceeded, my academic education. The formal and informal rituals and speeches and discussions about life and meaning left a bigger imprint than the formal classes about history and economics. Planning and participating in sit-ins and other civil rights activities were better political science and theory classes than even my very engaging professors Sam Cook and Howard Zinn could mount.

Students privately called Dr. Mays "Buck Bennie," lovingly mocked his words and mannerisms, and hungrily internalized his unerring belief that we were God's instruments for transforming the world.

Dr. Benjamin E. Mays was a remarkable man and role model for thousands of students who entered the doors of Morehouse, Spelman, Atlanta University, Clark, and Morris Brown Colleges, and the Inter-denominational Theological Seminary that constituted the broader Atlanta University center of Black higher education during his twenty-seven years of service as Morehouse's president. A mentor of mentors like Dr. Martin Luther King, Jr., Dr. Samuel DuBois Cook, Dr. Otis Moss, and Dr. Charles Adams, Benjamin Elijah Mays was born of slave parents in Ninety-Six, South Carolina and graduated from Bates College in Maine, where he didn't mind being an older student as he made up for lost time and earlier educational deprivation. He later earned his Ph.D. from the University of Chicago.

Ramrod straight of posture, unwaveringly principled and caring, keenly intelligent and elegant in speech, Dr. Mays inspired me with a passion for excellence and service as the following youthful poetic salute from my college diary attests.

> Tall Black man in flowing black robe
> stately beneath your snow crowned head
> trembling voice stirred with emotion
> eyes like magnets compelling my soul
> piercing words like darts shot from your
> heart to the enclosure of mine
> live forever, oh live forever.

Of the six college presidents in the Atlanta University academic complex, Dr. Mays was the one we looked up to most. He inspired and taught and stood by us when we challenged Atlanta's racial discrimination. Some of his teachings I wrote in my college diary. Others I internalized, and like many others who heard him frequently, I shared his words with others. I especially remember his oft-repeated "God's Minute" from an anonymous sage:

> I have just one minute
> Only sixty seconds in it,
> Forced upon me—can't refuse it
> Didn't seek it, didn't choose it,
> But it's up to me to use it.
> I must suffer if I lose it,
> Give account if I abuse it.
> Just a tiny little minute—
> But eternity is in it.

My dear friend Rev. Otis Moss, pastor of the Olivet Institutional Baptist Church in Cleveland, current chair of the Morehouse College Trustee Board, and former co-pastor with Rev. Martin Luther "Daddy" King, Sr., of Ebenezer Baptist church, described a meeting called by Daddy King to convince Martin Luther King, Jr., not to return to Montgomery. Like any parent, Daddy King did not want to see his child killed, hurt, or jailed. So he'd called together some of the best minds and friends in Atlanta to help convince his son to leave Montgomery. Dr. Mays was among them. When young Dr. King told the group that he would rather spend ten years in prison than abandon the people of Montgomery, Dr. Mays stood up to support him. And when Morehouse College gave the young Dr. King his first honorary degree and later, after his assassination, bade him farewell at a service on the grassy rectangle connecting Atlanta University with Morehouse where I stood with thousands of others, Dr. Mays movingly saluted his former student, fellow freedom fighter, and servant of God with Ralph Waldo Emerson's words: "See how the masses of men worry themselves into nameless graves, while here and there a great unselfish soul forgets himself into immortality."

How many high school and college students today are consistently urged to follow intrinsic rather than extrinsic values? Who is the morally authoritative voice among college presidents—Black, Brown, or White—for students of all races? Dr. Mays was a great unselfish soul who through the countless young people he inspired lives on. Today's prosperous America needs to heed his warning that "the tragedy of life is often not in our failure, but rather in our complacency; not in our doing too much, but rather in our doing too little; not in our living above our ability, but rather in our living below our capacities."

HOWARD ZINN

The tall, lanky professor and I arrived at Spelman College together in 1956. He and his wife Roslyn and their two children, Myla and Jeff, lived in the back of the Spelman College infirmary where students felt welcomed to gather, explore ideas, share hopes, and just chew the fat.

Howie encouraged students to think outside the box and to question rather than accept conventional wisdom. He was a risk-taker. I am indebted to him for my first interracial experience with a discussion group at the YMCA on international relations and for going with his Black Spelman students to sit in the "White" section of the state legislature which stopped its deliberations to hoot and jeer and demand that we be removed. He lost no opportunity to challenge segregation in theaters, libraries, and restaurants, and encouraged us to do the same.

Howie not only lived what he taught in history class by breaching Atlanta's segregated boundaries, but stretched my religious tolerance beyond childhood limits. I felt shock and confusion when he announced in class that he did not believe in Jesus Christ. There were few Jewish citizens in my small South Carolina hometown. Through him I began to discern that goodness comes in many faiths and forms which must be respected and honored.

The Black Spelman establishment did not like Howard Zinn any more than the White establishment did. Later, after he joined the faculty at Boston University, its president, John Silber, disliked him just as much as Spelman's president Albert Manley did, because he made some teachers and administrators uncomfortable by challenging the comfortable status quo. We called him Howie and felt him to be a confidant and friend as well as a teacher, contrary to the more formal and hierarchical traditions of many Black colleges. He stressed analysis and not memorization; questioning, discussions, and essays rather than multiple choices and pet answers; and he conveyed and affirmed my Daddy's belief and message that I could do and be anything and that life was about far more than bagging a Morehouse man for a husband.

He lived simply and nonmaterialistically. I felt comfortable asking to drive his old Chevrolet to transport picketers to Rich's department store. He was passionate about justice and his belief in the ability of individuals to make a difference in the world. Not a word-mincer, he said what he believed and encouraged us as students to do the same.

He conveyed to me and to other students that he believed in us. He conveyed to members of the Student Nonviolent Coordinating Committee whose voter registration and organizing efforts he chronicled in his book *SNCC: The New Abolitionists* that he believed in, respected, and supported our struggle. He was there when two hundred students conducted sit-ins and seventy-seven of us got arrested. He provided us a safe space in his home to plan civil rights activities by listening and not dictating. He laughed and enjoyed life just as he still does and he spoke up for the weak and little people against the big and powerful people just as he still does.

An eloquent chronicler of *The People's History of the United States,* of the Civil Rights Movement, and of the longings of the young and the poor and the weak to be free, his most profound message and the title of one of his books is that "you can't be neutral on a moving train." You can and must act against injustice.

Howie taught me to question and ponder what I read and heard and to examine and apply the lessons of history in the context of daily political, social, and moral challenges like racial discrimination and income inequality. He combined book learning with experiential opportunities to engage in interracial discussions; partnered with community groups challenging legal segregation; and engaged students as participants, observers, data collectors, and witnesses in pending legal cases as my diary recalls. He listened and answered questions as we debated strategies for conducting sit-in demonstrations to challenge segregated public dining facilities and used his car to check out, diagram, and help choreograph planned civil rights events. He reassured us of the rightness of our cause when uncertainty and fear crept in and some of our college presidents sought to dampen our spirits and discourage our activities.

In short, he was there for us through thick and thin, focused not just on our learning in the classroom but on our learning to stand up and feel empowered to act and change our own lives and the community and region in which we lived. He taught us to be neither victims nor passive observers of unjust treatment but active and proud claimants of our American birthright.

Howie helped prepare me to discover my leadership potential. With Charles Merrill, Howie made possible a defining year in my life by sending me as a nineteen-year-old Black girl from a small segregated southern town off to navigate the world of Europe all by myself.

I learned I could travel the world without losing my moral compass and common sense and not to fear, indeed to enjoy, being alone. I learned to be comfortable in strange lands with people who speak different languages, worship God in many different ways, have different political systems and ideologies and yet have the same human longing for freedom. Howard Zinn and Charles Merrill gave me a chance to get outside myself, outside segregated America, and roam around inside myself where one dreams, prays, and connects with our Creator and others.

Charles E. Merrill, Jr.

When I was eighteen years old and a sophomore at Spelman College, Charles E. Merrill, Jr., opened up the whole world to me. I'll never forget my fear upon being summoned to Spelman College President Albert Manley's office, wondering what infraction I'd been caught doing. And I'll never forget my elated disbelief at being told I'd been chosen as one of two Merrill Scholars—the greatest campus honor—providing a year of study and travel abroad. I ran back to my dorm in tears to call my Mama to share the exciting news which spread like wildfire throughout my hometown.

I thought how pleased my Daddy would be, as I still think at every accomplishment. I then ran to thank Howard Zinn who had nominated me. Soon Howie, Madame Billie Jeter Thomas, Spelman's elegant French department chair, and I began discussing where to go and with which group. Smith College and Sweet Briar College were among those offering structured academic and travel programs that lent social protection and guidance abroad. But Howard Zinn insisted that I not go with any group but travel on my own. This was a radical suggestion in the sheltered, planned-down-to-the-minute, closely supervised life of Spelman College.

Of Charles Merrill, Jr., I knew then only that he was privileged son of the founder of the Merrill Lynch brokerage house and brother of the poet James Merrill, who had invested his talents and wealth in developing young people. Impressed with the confidence and pride of Morehouse men he had met in the army, Charles Merrill, Jr., later sought out Morehouse College and Dr. Benjamin E. Mays. He eventually chaired Morehouse's Board of Trustees. His lasting contributions include founding the Commonwealth School in Boston and establishing the Merrill Fellowship for a year's travel and study abroad for Morehouse students which he later, thank goodness, extended to one Spelman student in 1957 and then two in 1958. I was one of the lucky two. That year changed my life and Charles Merrill's friendship enriched it.

Charles Merrill did not just give a scholarship; he gave himself in long conversations, letters, and visits. He became a lifelong friend whose confidence and expectations I wanted to live up to and reciprocate. I still do.

He shared time and advice and books including Orwell's *1984* and the *Road to Wigan Pier* that remain on my bookshelves still. He responded regularly to my long excited ramblings during my year abroad and promptly set me straight by return mail when I wrote him about my conversations with a young former German Nazi soldier whose charm and agony momentarily clouded my moral accountability thermometer at a youth camp in the Soviet Union. Painfully shy but keenly interested in my youthful perceptions and experiences, his investment in sending students abroad multiplied throughout our college and home communities as Merrill Scholars shared impressions and reports upon returning from the big free world of Europe.

After graduating from Spelman I would visit Charles and Mary Merrill's home on Commonwealth Avenue in Boston, their farm in New Hampshire, and occasionally the Commonwealth School in Boston, where he served as headmaster for many years. When I was in law school, he visited me in New Haven, treated me to a play and dinner, and came to Mississippi, where he applauded my ability not just to try civil rights cases but to competently cook an egg sunny side up for breakfast. He later served on CDF's board and made me as proud as a child by attending every one of my five W. E. B. DuBois lectures at Harvard in the 1980s, then coming to hear me in Boston when my book, *The Measure of Our Success*, was published.

Children and adults never cease needing the approval of their mentors. In opening up the whole world to me—a nineteen-year-old Black girl forty-one years ago—Charles Merrill in turn opened it up to my three sons who travel comfortably all over the world today and recognize the common humanity of God in all peoples regardless of language, geography, color, ideology, or nationality.

Many ask today whether Black children and youth can benefit from White role models and mentors. Of course they can. While children certainly need mentors with whom they can identify personally from common experiences of race, gender, culture, and economic circumstance, they also need to be shown and taught that human values and caring know no racial or gender boundaries: that all people have something to teach and learn; that race and class need not prevent sharing and helping; and that every person is our neighbor and every child our charge. Charles Merrill enabled me to learn that lesson which I shared with my Spelman sisters when I returned home for my senior year. Speaking in Sisters Chapel I said:

> By getting a glimpse into the lives of others, I have come to examine my own life much more closely. I have come to see my place as an individual

in the world community. I have come to know my own worth—my own importance. I have burst out of the old bonds of provincialism which had once so limited me, and have been made to feel the needs— not just of Spelman, the South, and America—but of the whole world. I have become an individual aware of personal and national shortcomings, and determined to correct these in every instance offered me. I have seen and felt the sufferings of others and gained incentive to alleviate it in my own small way.

I realize that I am not fighting just for myself, or my people in the South, when I fight for freedom and equality. I realize now that I fight for the moral and political health of America as a whole and for her position in the world at large. I see that I aid the African and the Asian in their struggle for self-realization by my example as I push the cause of freedom a step further by gaining my own. I know that I show the Communist that one can advance in a democratic society. I know that I, in my individual struggle for improvement, help the world. I am no longer an isolated being—I belong. Europe helped me to see this!

There were many other inspiring teachers and preachers during my Spelman years who befriended me, guided me, and shared the struggle for racial justice. M. Carl Holman was a Clark College professor and poet who later moved to Washington to become Deputy Director of the U.S. Civil Rights Commission, President of the National Urban Coalition, and my son Jonah's godfather. Dr. Samuel DuBois Cook, of whom I gushed in my diary, "I'm in love with his mind," was a professor of political theory at Atlanta University and later president of Dillard University, a disciple of Dr. Mays, and a gifted teacher. Howard Zinn thought I'd gain greatly from taking one of Sam's graduate courses in political theory. He was right. I basked in the imaginative challenges of Sam Cook's classes as he invited us to construct visions of a future world order through the ideas, beliefs, and lives of Gandhi, Tolstoy, Trotsky, Bakunin, Lenin, Martin Luther King, Jr., and others.

I thank Sam Cook for prodding me to try to see and feel the world through the eyes of others and to open my mind to and digest a variety of ideas and attempt to apply them to the life and circumstances around me. He helped me eschew doctrinaire rigidity, and he, like

Howard Zinn, was always there with the bottom-line question: How will a position help or hurt others or bend the universe closer to justice?

Esta Seaton taught me English at Spelman, and she and her musician husband Danny provided warmth, intellectual stimulation, and friendship. Howard Thurman, Langston Hughes, E. Franklin Frazier, and other great speakers who visited Spelman's campus all created a climate of can-do and must-serve in us.

But three names are entered over and over in my college diary and mind's eye: Dr. Mays, Charles Merrill, and Howard Zinn. Like my Daddy, they reinforced in me a sense that I could transcend the world I lived in and help transform it into the world I wanted to see. They taught the oneness of humankind and shared a passion for justice and excellence. They empowered me to make a difference. I thank them and hope to pass on their torch to those coming behind.

❧ 5 ❧
EUROPE

❦

WHEN I WOKE UP on my first morning in Paris on my Merrill Fellowship and looked out of my window at teeming crowds on Boulevard St. Michel below and the beautiful Luxembourg Gardens across the street, I jumped up and down and yelled and pinched myself again and again. Having no one, parent or teacher or chaperone, to prescribe the day was a man-made miracle of Howard Zinn and Charles Merrill. I was nineteen and on my own—free—for the first time in my life!

In the first months away from home and Spelman's gated community, I could not believe that I could go wherever I wanted, when I wanted, and do whatever I wanted. I have always loved exploring and wandering off the beaten track with no set destination for hours and hours and whole days. I roamed Paris streets, alleys, nooks, and crannies unafraid, hungrily drinking up sights and sounds and smells and people and art and history and differences with uncontained excitement. I would sit for long spells in the Luxembourg Gardens reading and watching the children's sailboats. Sitting in a public garden was a new experience for me and I soon learned to relax and enjoy it. I had known no public spaces like that in America's South and am so mindful now of the importance of beautiful spaces for the nourishment of the spirit and of the mind. I thought nothing about getting up one morning and traveling alone to Ireland to walk in the countryside near Dublin and then traveling to roam the streets of Belfast, and later Glasgow and Edinburgh in Scotland. I loved exploring the fairytale city of Edinburgh, listening to the great Zagreb Solisti String Quartet, and going to concert after concert after concert during the Edinburgh music festival. I first experienced Pablo Casals and the great guitarist Andrés Segovia in Europe. I caught a train to Spain to experience a bullfight, which I hated, but I basked in El Greco's Toledo and Madrid's Prado museum. I found I loved being alone to read and daydream. In Paris, I would haunt places where Victor Hugo and Zola had walked, and every time I walked across one of the Seine's bridges I put myself in the skin of Camus' disengaged protagonist in *The Fall*, a defining book in my life. I read Colette and D. H. Lawrence and Sartre and Frantz Fanon and hung out where Richard Wright and other self-exiled Black artists gathered.

At the International Student Hostel at 93 Boulevard St. Michel where I stayed and at the Sorbonne where I took a summer course in French civilization, I met young people from all over the world. The 1956 Hungarian Revolution had flooded Western Europe with young political exiles. My roommate came from Uruguay. Hours of dialogue with African counterparts made me realize the commonality of our freedom struggle but also how much America not Africa was my home. How proud I was of Dr. Martin Luther King, Jr., and of Mrs. Rosa Parks and the swelling challenges to American apartheid back home. In Paris, I engaged in long, honest interracial conversations with southern White students who like me were seeking to reconcile the chasm between America's professed principles of equality and freedom and its actual practices.

In Europe, wellsprings of long-suppressed rage bubbled up within me against the confining prison of segregation my native South and country had imposed. I knew I'd never return to that prison again either as a Black citizen or as a woman. No one would ever again define my place or what I could achieve or be on the basis of race and gender.

I can't stand routines and bureaucracies that stifle individual creativity and possibility. I bristle at the immoral, unfair, and blanket sorting of children, especially children to whom life's lottery has dealt a tough hand, by adults or peers who write them off as "underprivileged" or "inner city" or "under-achievers" or "disabled" or "geeks" and therefore worthless by prevailing societal measures. Since I did not realize what I could not do, I tried everything time and opportunity permitted. I managed to learn enough French to pass my courses at the Sorbonne and later in Geneva and took a year of Russian so that I could greet the Russian people whom I was determined to visit before returning home. Tolstoy's writings had profoundly affected me as a college student, especially *The Kingdom of God Is Within You, What Men Live By, Where Love Is There God Is*, and *The Death of Ivan Ilyich*.

Thanks to Howie Zinn's insistence that I not be boxed in by a prescribed program, I could and did decide that I could stretch my dollars to stay in Europe for fifteen rather than twelve months—two summers and an academic year—if I went to the University of Geneva in Switzerland rather than remaining at the Sorbonne. Geneva was cheaper and had a graduate school of international relations which I thought would help me explore my then career dream of entering the Foreign Service.

I lived frugally and saved every possible penny from my $3,000 Merrill Fellowship so I could not only attend the University for the school year but also participate in a six-week Lisle Fellowship student exchange to the Soviet Union. My savings from scrimping, some scholarship help from Lisle, and, I now know, sacrificial help from my mother, who sold two small pieces of property my father had left her, made the latter trip possible.

I squeezed in a summer seminar at Lincoln College at Oxford University before the academic year in Geneva. At Oxford, I stayed at St. Hilda's College, walked the beautiful grounds of Balliol College where our summer seminar coordinator was a student, and attended classes at Lincoln College with young people from around the world. I marveled at God's graceful circles when I returned to Balliol for my son Jonah's graduation when he earned his doctorate as a Rhodes Scholar and we attended a luncheon given him by his tutors at Lincoln College. The sense that all is planned by a Higher Being returns to me often.

In Geneva, my three American roommates and I shared two rooms. Our first rental was with a Russian countess who had known Leo Tolstoy and his wife, and who railed about what a terrible husband he was. My roommates and I rebelled when the countess tried to re-institute Spelman in Geneva by imposing rigid strictures and routines on our lives—teatimes, expectations about conversation (which, I now recognize, were simply a lonely old woman's need for company), and curfews. After a few months the four of us decided to split up and move around the corner. I lived with a Swiss woman who befriended us but kept a more hands-off stance with her college-age American charges testing their wings. The nearby John Knox House headed by Paul Frelich was a haven for fellowship and meals. I liked my roommates very much, and the four of us continued to be friends and to travel together during school breaks. My French would have been much improved, however, by not rooming with Americans!

Two other friendships provided encouragement, familylike meals, and stability during my stimulating Geneva schoolyear. Vivian and Joe Young, Black Americans, provided a home away from home. Joe worked for the International Labor Organization (ILO) and Vivian was a full-time mother to all young newcomers. She shepherded me and Roslyn Pope—the other Spelman Merrill Scholar—through Italy and up to her quiet Swiss chalet where she still returns every summer. It is a source of enormous satisfaction for me that Vivian, now over seventy-five, working with Joe and their son, Butch, heads Stand for Children in Delaware and shares with children the same warmth, advocacy, and support she did with me as a young Black college student in a strange land. Vivian came to my Spelman College graduation and has remained a constant presence in my life even when we do not see each other regularly. On my first day at Yale Law School, I met a young restless Black man at Yale's graduate school who was uncertain about what he wanted to do with his life. I advised him to leave Yale and go to Geneva to see Vivian. He was Donald Stewart, who later became president of Spelman College and head of the College Board. Later it was my pleasure to broker a marriage between Donald and the lovely Isabelle Johnston whom I'd met on a summer Crossroads Africa project in the Ivory Coast. Isabelle now heads Girls, Inc., which provides mentors for young girls.

My other Geneva friendship was with Liliane Jacot-Descombes, a wonderful Swiss nurse who became like a sister. She had fallen in love with Finley Campbell, a Merrill Scholar from Morehouse whose Detroit preacher father, Dynamo Campbell, had run revival meetings in my father's church and whose family often stayed with our family. Liliane was a sturdy anchor who accompanied me to and literally pushed me through the door for the scary oral exams in French at the University of Geneva when I froze, convinced I was going to flunk. She moved to Atlanta the following year, married Finley, who was teaching at Morehouse, and adopted two interracial children, who are now grown and living in Geneva, where she returned after their divorce.

I did pass my exams administered by three stern examiners. When I was done, I hitchhiked with a young Black woman friend from Geneva to Hamburg, Germany to meet my Lisle Fellowship group and then took a train to Warsaw, Poland en route to the Soviet Union. Hitchhiking was the one experience I probably would not repeat. My Daddy always cautioned against it at home but in Europe it was and is safer and Karen and I arrived sound, untouched, and on time after rides mostly with truck drivers. We did question our judgment after accepting a ride from two young motorcyclists who misread our intentions and tested our wills when they went off the highway into an empty field. Protest and prayer delivered us from what they perceived as a sexual invitation. My friend returned home to America and I met Rev. William Keys, my Lisle leader, and the group, which included a big, brown, beautiful Spelman student, Virginia Powell, whom the Russians would stop, stare, and point at as if she were a Black princess, and one brilliant Black man from Washington, D.C., Henry Robinson. In Warsaw I called a Polish friend, Stephan Durski, whom I'd met at Lincoln College at Oxford. Stephan picked me up, drove me with his friends to the ocean many miles away, and returned me to Warsaw at the crack of dawn barely in time to catch the train to the Soviet Union with my frantic group and leader.

The summer of 1959 in the Soviet Union was magical. I experienced the American Exhibition in Moscow, one of the windows being opened into the Iron Curtain that made possible student exchanges like mine. I witnessed the exciting Khrushchev–Nixon debate from a few yards' distance; met Carl Sandburg whose multivolume biography of Lincoln my Daddy had bought for us when we were children; and debated with Moscow University students and other Soviet citizens but always in carefully arranged settings. We danced with warm and stout Soviet women at a youth camp near Sochi in the Caucasus (the war had killed millions of Russian men), roamed with crowds of Russian peasants through the priceless treasures of the Hermitage in Leningrad and saw the Tsars' beautiful dwellings at Petrograd. In addition to wanting to visit Tolstoy's home, Yasnaya Polyana, I had hoped to find and meet Dr. W. E. B. DuBois in the Soviet Union, but by that time he had moved to Ghana. And I look forward still to going to Tolstoy's home.

The Soviet Union's constraints on thought and daily life made me bristle just as I did in the segregated South. I left with no illusion about Communism.

A chance personal meeting with Khrushchev and the president of Czechoslovakia topped off the summer. Our Lisle student group was visiting a rural Russian village near the Black Sea resort of Sochi when three big cars drove up and out stepped Premier Nikita Khrushchev, the president of Czechoslovakia, and other dignitaries. The villagers brought out bottles of vodka and large glasses with which we engaged in toasts one after another as we danced and sang and celebrated the leaders' presence. I took the first drink of my life. My teetotaling family had been influenced by my Baptist daddy's anti-alcohol stricture, but also by a family predilection to alcoholism that ravaged the lives of three of my maternal uncles and later two of my brothers. My brother Arthur overcame it and made a wonderful contribution to other recovering alcoholics as head of an alcohol and drug rehabilitation center in Brooklyn; my brother Julian's productive life as a teacher and caretender for the elderly was cut short. Good manners, I thought, precluded my refusing huge refills as I got happily drunk for the first time in my life. I was less happy the next day!

I loved the Russian people and learned that summer to distinguish between them and their political rulers whom I did not love or trust. Attending a Baptist church service and hearing the mournful songs

and moving harmony, I felt as at home as I did in Black Baptist
churches in the South. Similar feelings of home washed over me decades later attending a church service in Addis Ababa, Ethiopia,
crammed with mothers bearing babies and old men leaning on prayer
sticks amidst ancient but somehow familiar prayer and musical chants
and rhythms.

I could never return home to a segregated South and a constraining
Spelman College in the same way. After wandering the world, sharing
the struggles for liberation of Hungarian, African, and Iranian students, sensing the longing for freedom of my Soviet student guides
and counterparts who secretly shared their fears and frustrations, dis-
cerning the common thread of God in my fellow human beings, the
genie of freedom could not be put back into the bottle of racial and
gender segregation in America. As I reluctantly returned home to a
changing South, the Civil Rights Movement and Dr. King were poised
to give a powerful outlet to my longings.

While I was in Europe, Dr. King had been stabbed in the chest by a
mentally ill woman in Harlem. I prayed hard for him and thought
years later about this period in my life and his, including his recupera-
tion in Rev. Sandy Ray's home on President Street in Brooklyn, the
parsonage of the Cornerstone Baptist Church where my brother
Harry, Rev. Sandy Ray's successor, now lives. When I visit Harry I
sleep in the bedroom where Martin Luther King, Jr., healed before
returning to southern battlegrounds to forge a more racially just
America.

Home again after more than a year abroad, I was eager to share my
experiences and to help transform my homeland. I had missed my
mother greatly and loved returning to report back to my Black home
community that had sent me off with much pride and prayers. My
brother Harry, who had succeeded my Daddy as pastor of Shiloh Baptist Church in 1954, met me at the dock in Quebec on my return home
from Europe. When he told our Shiloh congregation on my first Sunday back how I had ordered lunch for the two of us in Quebec in
French, the congregation responded with a loud warm hum of pride.
I was home.

MARTIN LUTHER KING, JR., AND A SPRING OF CHANGE

T HIS LETTER, dated March 4, 1997, carrying a return address of "The Master's House, Trumbull College, Yale University" arrived on my desk bringing a great gift of memories from the past.

Dear Ms. Edelman,

This package will come as a surprise to you. Let me explain how it came to be in my hands.

In 1987 we moved from the chaplain's house, 66 Wall Street, to Trumbull College. While packing I came across this notebook which I had never seen before. I read enough to see it was a diary from a student at Spelman. I'm a journal keeper myself, so I felt sure the owner would like to have this. I tossed it in a box for High Street, expecting to write Spelman for an address once I could decipher this name on the front of the notebook. Now, ten years later, we are packing to leave Trumbull College. I was sorting out books yesterday and came across this mystery notebook again. Thumbing through it I said to Harry: "This woman may be famous today. Look, she says she plans to go to Harvard. And listen to this beautiful prayer."

Another flip of the pages and I read your impression of meeting Martin Luther King. I asked Harry to look at the name on the front. (I could make out only Elizabeth Wright.) "It says Marian Elizabeth Wright," he noted. Then suddenly: "It must be Marian Wright Edelman!" We were both overjoyed at this discovery.

I felt sudden guilt for having read parts of something so private. However, I am glad I did. It is truly providential.

Sincerely,

Manette Adams

(Mrs. Harry Baker Adams)

The diary of my senior year at Spelman chronicles my youthful struggles to re-enter the segregated world of America's South and of Spelman's gated gentility after Europe. And it shows how the Civil Rights Movement gave powerful and timely voice to my yearning to be free.

I did not return home the same person who had left. The new wine of freedom and self-confidence could not be poured back into the old wineskin of the Jim Crow South or into the traditional confines of what a Black woman could aspire to in America. I did not know how I would make the metamorphosis into the new person laboring to be born, as the ensuing diary excerpts attest, but I knew I would.

No words have been changed from the excerpted diary portions that appear throughout this chapter. However, many pages describing my infatuation with a Morehouse man who I can now barely remember have been mercifully omitted!

I apologize if I embarrass any of my mentors here with my heartfelt youthful feelings. Rereading my diary after nearly forty years reaffirmed for me how much adults really matter to young people and the power they have to mold them for good or ill in ways they cannot foresee. Parents, teachers, leaders: pay attention. In an era in which mentoring has become increasingly professionalized or left to volunteers, these important supplemental programs and individual efforts are not substitutes for the daily adult examples in children's lives. The most important mentoring is not primarily about a few hours a week or month of volunteer time with a child. It is who we are and what we do and say every day in our homes, classrooms, work places, congregations, cultural, civic, and political lives that children absorb to develop their sense of worth.

The following portions of the diary from November 1959 through April 1960 reflect a period of (occasionally self-absorbed!) torment and topsy-turvy emotions and mood changes. I had spent the early fall reporting on my fellowship year to my college community, starting a mentoring program for younger Spelman sisters, and frantically trying to decide on a major and a minor. I had a number of hours in international relations, which Spelman did not offer as a major, and in other courses like Russian history that I had enjoyed in Europe, but not enough in a single subject to meet Spelman's requirements. I decided on social science as a major and English as a minor and had a wonderful time reading novels alone in a cozy third-floor dorm room without a roommate. And I'm sure I hold Spelman's record for most games bowled in a week. After my junior year abroad, I had to make up two of the six required semesters in physical education before graduation. So I took bowling and swimming. The latter was compulsory. Although I was not a swimmer as a result of a childhood experience of nearly drowning, I did what I had to do to pass Spelman's swimming test. I do love water aerobics in shallow pools. I do not swim.

My diary of these first few months back at Spelman show me casting about for my calling and a cause. Both would become dramatically clear to me soon into the new year.

NOVEMBER 20, 1959

I've gotten away from the old me so I have been left to create and find a new me. What must God think of me? I've stopped going to church for the first time in my life—the services bore me. There's not enough challenge. I've been spending the time praying, reading, and meditating alone. . . . I wish I knew what I was looking for. . . . I wish I had a great, great mind—one that would create me a real world that I could flee to. As it is, I am left at the mercy of the common fold. I've thought about suicide but what would Mama do? Made *Who's Who* —wanted to—now it seems so unimportant. What petty things we crave. What lowly loads weigh our minds and lives down.

What a turn my life has taken. What a difference Europe has made. What a new world of possibility and destination has opened up to me. It'll be interesting to watch it unfolding.

DECEMBER 4, 1959

I spoke in Morehouse's Chapel and it went very well. What a pleasant shock I got just before going up to the rostrum. In walked Harry, Chequita, and Debbie [my brother, his wife, and baby daughter]. I was thunderstruck. Father and Mama Scott were there and Dr. Barksdale was there and Sam Cook came. [The Scotts published the *Atlanta Daily World*, Dr. Barksdale taught English at Morehouse, and Sam Cook was a professor at Atlanta University.] Got a very warm reception and was not in the least nervous astoundingly enough.

DECEMBER 9, 1959

This has been a wonderfully enjoyable and enlightening day—wish all days were like this! Had two-hour talk with Mr. Peterson—a colored from South Africa touring the states on an education exchange between our two countries. After he spoke in chapel, I went backstage to arrange an appointment and was not impressed by his speech and was outraged by what he did not say. Mentioned next to nothing about South Africa. Today I went to jump down his throat—and what a lesson I learned! He taught me a profound lesson in tactics—about not committing suicide when there's a job to be done: to let your reason, not your emotions, govern. He has made headway in South Africa not by unleashed radicalism but by careful and subtle calculations—knowing the enemies and rendering their tools impotent. Had recently won prize for writing and had great faith in pen. He told me when I get furious with myself and the world—to sit down and let the pen fly. One sublimates—can fight—in secret with self and here is where one can hide from the world. Also advised, "Never speak in absolutes. Keep the opponent guessing—be wise in what you say by not having to say it!"

Mr. Merrill in town, hope I can see him before we meet formally at the Manleys. [Dr. Albert E. Manley was president of Spelman.]

Yesterday, I and several others in social science club went down to court. Case of segregation with Dobbs House restaurant in the airport was being contested. We were to serve as witnesses for we'd surveilled it, counting Negro frequenters of airport. I was not expecting to be a witness but my name was called to stand by. Howie says case looks good for us but one never knows . . .

Bless Mama and make me fit for whatever Thou would have me do Lord.

DECEMBER 11, 1959

I just came back from Morehouse's chapel where I heard Mr. Merrill speak. He's a shy and modest man. Strode up to the stage head down, hands folded behind his back. He seems always to be in deep thought. He reminisced about postwar Europe and the Nuremberg Trials and the utter chaos all around him. Recalled walking down Nuremberg streets where all the buildings had been desolated and seeing several women coming out of building talking about teatime and finding it unimaginable that anybody could occupy themselves with such trivia. He came to realize later the worth of it—for two human beings to maintain the sense of dailiness amid destruction—the courage to keep going—pretend until the reality around you can be rebuilt. Education, why education, he asked? To make you more fit to live, to share, to help find oneself. "Because life's a one-way street—a one-time job. You must make the very best of it." And he abruptly sat.

Dr. Mays got up and announced that Morehouse was going to honor Mr. Merrill for his thirteen years of service to Morehouse. Went up afterwards to shake hands with him. Dr. Mays presented me and mentioned my town meeting report on Russia. Mr. Merrill affirmed he knew it was fine because those last two letters were as fine as anything he'd ever read by anybody. I was overwhelmed. I am going to write him to ask about my current thoughts and problems because I know he'll understand. Please, God, help him to understand how grateful I am to him for what he's done for me but above that, for what he is.

DECEMBER 12, 1959

I had a talk with Mr. Merrill at Dr. Mays' house this morning. We talked for an hour and he walked me back to Spelman. I told him about what I want to do and asked his advice. He saw the need for leadership. I told him about my dilemma of choosing between law and international relations. I can see he seemed inclined towards international work and tried to wrangle a way that I could possibly combine both.

I asked him about the medium or gradient level to be established between serving self and others. My fear and scorn of all humanity and desire to run away from it—withdraw. He told me a little story whose essence was: take the best of humanity—pick out the part that is changeable and susceptible to betterment and change it. Overlook the rest. Grab the thread of hope from the whole cloth and make it one of quality—work with whatever there is to work with and let the rest go.

I learned more about him this morning. That he'd quit Harvard after his second year because he couldn't stand the regularities of life while the war was on. He worked on a collective farm in Mississippi; knows how others feel because he's made it a point to get down with them and share their suffering. He feels very deeply. Talked about his impressions of Thurgood Marshall whom he had heard speak in Boston. Personally, he dislikes his manner which is theatrical and gushing and overfamiliar, but when Thurgood Marshall began to speak, his persona, ability, and knowledge commanded unsurmounted respect. He's a man whose knowledge is thoroughly based in the scope of American history.

When I asked about continuing to correspond with him because I felt he understands me and I wanted to use him as a sounding board—he immediately and very graciously assented.

What more need one ask of life than to be made aware of the earth underneath, towering trees overhead, songs of birds which fill the air—of the grass bending with the sway of the wind—of the sky with its curtains of clouds drawn partially to show the rising moon for the night, and which play the scenes of the setting colors of the sun as it gives its last bloody breath. What more could one ask than to feel the throb of his fellow man and to share his brothers' misery—feel his problems to be his own—sing with him. Fall astray and wander back amid the thorn and thistles of life to the clearing together—to struggle to be sensitive to the needs of others—to feel life every second—to stay away from commonplaces—lethargy—to never be caught one minute unthinking—to feel deeply—have a highly developed inner life—to find self so that I can commune with me—to love—to have a self that can't be taken away—undergirded with the precepts of our Lord Jesus Christ. To be caring, venturesome, questing, brave, fearless, pugnacious, persisting, unrelenting, humble, grateful—to be genuine, sincere, grateful, honest and truthful. Thank you God for a Charles Merrill, Howard Zinn, and Benjamin Mays.

DECEMBER 14, 1959

God, what am I to do? This morning I definitely decided to become a civil rights lawyer and I've been thinking about it fiercely the whole day. Worrying about getting into Yale where I definitely want to go. I talked to Mama tonight and she threw any hints of the idea down the drain—wants me to get my masters and work. I owe her a lot—but also my people. "You can do whatever you will after I'm gone." She feels she won't live long and wants to see me settled. She understands me not at all! There is no source of intellectual, spiritual, and emotional help in my family. They don't seem to realize what a fiercely competitive world we live in. What am I to do Lord? How can I show her what I must do without hurting Mama? God, how can I expose to her the bigness and necessity of my vision? I see now that the only way I'll go to law school is by scholarship and work beginning this summer. Europe's over and hard grim reality is now in. You've got such a fight. To whom do I owe my life? To Mama, to self, to Howard Zinn, to Spelman, to Charles Merrill, the Negro, to my country, to Thee? All of these I must please but ultimately—and above all—Thee. God make me strong in purpose, will, and goodness. Show me what I must do and help me to unfalteringly do it. Help my family to understand.

DECEMBER 17, 1959

Got a card from Mr. Merrill thanking me for the record and saying how much he enjoyed the visit. Gave such a lift to my day! To think that he takes time out to write and so promptly. I hope we will be really good friends later on.

My freshman group is to put on several performances at the federal penitentiary tomorrow evening. God, please help us to reach the audience—to entertain as well as relay a message. Keep us safe.

DECEMBER 24, 1959

Christmas Eve at home. I've been thinking this evening of my last Christmas Eve. I had left Geneva with M.T., Sue, and Lucie for the Riviera and we spent the night at Les Baux en Provence—the coldest and clearest night of my life. How good God has been to me. How much He lets me see, hear, and feel. How much more is there promise of. What a big wide diverse world this is. He has allowed me to be relieved of the regular small town rut and made me see what life can be like. I'm craving—shimmering—expectant—excited about what life holds. I want to seek its very essences. I want to be good in it and to it.

DECEMBER 25, 1959

It is Christmas. What do I feel? Christ—where art Thou? Where is love and peace and understanding? We are so unworthy. Help us to be fit and clean for Thee. Right in our seeking, pure in our thoughts, and loving in our actions.

Thank you for Jesus Christ. Help me to be worthy of Thy great gift, my Mama, sister, and brothers.

Mama and I argued about my career. She isn't taken with the notion of law school but will let me do what I want to do. I'm on my own.

I walked the streets of Bennettsville the other night up through the square and read the inscriptions of the monuments—the big statue to Johnny Reb and others who died to maintain another people in bondage and are praised for it. We worship our death and corruption. The very things that bring us low we cherish. What strange and wayward creatures we men are.

I hope that Mama and I might understand each other. She's done an awful lot for me. God help me to repay her tenfold in accomplishments.

America—what mean you to me? I long and pine for Europe—to abandon all restraint, to think all thoughts, express all ideas; to be me—any kind of me I feel the need to be; to wrangle forcefully—to fight over opinions and to judge. I finished Sartre's *L'Age de Raison*. Powerful. Depressing. Life can be so ugly, yet it can be so fine, full, and worthwhile. This is what we seek.

JANUARY 7, 1960

Went to hear May Sarton talk about her writing. Have been rather happy these last few days. Reading and sticking to myself. Yesterday began reading Gide's *The Immoralist*. Finished it this morning. "The writer does not write to tell but to learn, to search. A novelist should feel rather than know."

Getting into and living yourself the life of the characters is great. Am going to read Ruskin this week. Must prepare diligently for my exams. God help my mind to be true and craving always—set at awe in the light of truth—always looking and searching to know about everything.

Make my will like iron, Lord—ever drumming against the hard facade of reality. Make me honest and persistent in my quest for life—always seeking the deep—the high while not overlooking the simple. I feel as if I am a stranger to myself these days. I startle myself at my audacity and am outraged by my timidity. I hate my weaknesses. I am frustrated by my limitations. I fear my thoughts of Thee. Without You I dare not nor desire to live. Man is not enough. I fear that I am losing Thee God. I am drifting. I feel guilty and lost. Forgive my waywardness and show me the way back to Thee.

JANUARY 20, 1960

Try to be worthy, Marian. Never fear. Never worry. Think on God and His will. You are nothing without Him. Seek His guidance and make your ears susceptible to His biddings. "In all Thy ways acknowledge Him, and He will direct Thy path." God is good to me. Far above my desert. He has allowed me the presence of a Benjamin Mays and Charles Merrill, a Peterson from South Africa; a Poole from Holland.

Look high. Gaze amidst the stars and be dazzled by their light. Temptations have beset me on all sides—I am forced to flee from my self's vanities and deceits. I have seen mass hypocrisy and devastating shallowness. Help me to be high in thought, high in deed, Lord. Fear nothing and realize that our whole duty and privilege is to Thee.

♦

My yearnings and confusions coalesced powerfully by spring of 1960 in the student sit-in movement. Although Dr. Martin Luther King had entered my consciousness and heart in 1955 and 1956 as the voice of the Montgomery bus boycott, I personally heard him speak for the first time on April 19, 1960 in Spelman's Sisters Chapel during my senior year. His mother and sister Christine King Farris had attended Spelman and Christine taught at Spelman for many years. Dr. King had graduated from nearby Morehouse College, whose president, during his college days and mine, was the indomitable Benjamin Elijah Mays.

The profound impact on me of hearing Dr. King that first time is evident in my diary where I repeated long portions of his speech that had vibrated the chords of my freedom- and justice-hungry soul.

It is not often that great leaders and great turning points in history converge and sweep us up in a movement. My generation was blessed beyond measure to be in the right places at the right times to experience and help bring transforming change to the South and to America in partnership with mentor-leaders like Dr. King, seeking to serve God and a cause bigger than ourselves.

Black students had been galvanized by the February 1, 1960 sitdown demonstration by four Black A&T (Agricultural and Technical State College) students at a Woolworth's lunch counter in Greensboro, North Carolina. They had nonviolently withstood the abusive behavior of White hooligans with dignity and persistence as they returned each day. Many Black students in Atlanta and elsewhere were equally ready to strike our blow for freedom.

In March, student leaders and the student body president from each of the Black colleges making up the Atlanta University Center—Morehouse, Spelman, Clark, Morris Brown, Atlanta University, and the Interdenominational Theological Center—signed "An Appeal for

Human Rights." It was published in full-page ads on March 9, 1960 in the *Atlanta Constitution, Atlanta Journal*, and *Atlanta Daily World*.

The Appeal stated that "every normal human being wants to walk the earth with dignity and abhors any and all proscriptions upon him because of race or color. In essence, this is the meaning of the sit-down protests that are sweeping this nation today. We do not intend to wait placidly for those rights which are ours already legally and morally to be meted out to us one at a time. We want to state clearly and unequivocally that we cannot tolerate, in a nation professing democracy and among people professing Christianity, the discriminatory conditions under which the Negro is living today." The appeal detailed the gross inequalities and discrimination in education, jobs, housing, voting, hospitals, movies, concerts, restaurants, and law enforcement.

After calling on all the adults in authority of all races and on all leaders in civic life—ministers, teachers, and business people—"and all people of good will to exert themselves and abolish those general injustices," we announced our "plans to use every legal and nonviolent means at our disposal to secure full citizenship rights as members of this great Democracy of ours."

Students had carefully drafted the ad at the behest of our college presidents who had gained a whiff of our "secret" meetings at Yates and Milton's corner drugstore near our campuses where we were planning sit-downs like the highly publicized ones in Greensboro. While very mixed in their attitudes towards their students' impatience and plans to protest against segregation, my college diary says, "There was one place where we were all together: the need for clarity of purpose." Morehouse president Dr. Benjamin E. Mays told an Atlanta University audience years later, "Before the students did anything, we wanted to make it clear what they were striking about or grumbling about or protesting about." The presidents not only provided the money to pay for the ads (a freedom that private, unlike public, colleges could exercise), but they also read it and were in full accord with it. The evidence for this is plain from a slip of paper with scribbled notes concerning the Appeal that also includes comments from Dr. Mays that fell from my college diary thirty-seven years after I'd put it there. Dr. Mays' comments on the Appeal call it a "great document" that sets forth a philosophy and makes the case in a manner that "nobody has said the same way."

We students believed in the Appeal and the meaning behind it with our whole minds and bodies and souls and were prepared to go to jail and even to die for those beliefs. The response to the eloquent student appeal was loud and mixed. Georgia's segregationist Governor Vandiver claimed it was a "Communist-inspired document and that students couldn't have written it." I recalled his comment in an Aspen Institute Seminar in the 1970s when a corporate executive questioned whether Dr. King had really written "A Letter from a Birmingham Jail." Some White students issued statements of support of our Black student appeal.

We followed up the Appeal by sitting in on March 15, 1960 at seven White-only restaurants in Atlanta. I and seventy-seven other students were arrested on that day for our actions. Our series of demonstrations included a boycott of Rich's department store in Atlanta (we incorrectly calculated its prominent Jewish owners would be more sympathetic to ending discrimination because of the Jews' history of persecution not realizing the equally likely psychological reaction to protect one's own perceived unsecured status which is what happened). Student pressure eventually led to an Atlanta Compromise: seventy-five stores officially opened up 177 counters to Black citizens. Atlanta became the 104th city to desegregate lunch counters since the sit-ins began in February 1960, but the legal pressures and charges were still pending in various places and remained to be settled. The U.S. Supreme Court accepted a case involving sit-in students like me in 1964. I got out of law school in time to help write the brief.

Dr. King's message at Spelman in April that "segregation is a cancer killing democracy's health" affirmed and emboldened us. From April 19, 1960, until his assassination on April 4, 1968, he was a continuous, personal, important presence in my life and in that of so many other young people. His courageous example, his accessibility to me and to other young people in the movement, and his support at a time when only a few of our professors—Howard Zinn at Spelman, M. Carl Holman at Clark College (later president of the National Urban Coalition), Whitney Young, Dean of Atlanta University's School of Social Work (later president of the National Urban League)—openly supported us was incalculably important.

Young people need the example and validation of adults they respect when they are trying to do the right thing especially when it is unpopular. We needed to be encouraged to take risks and not to be deterred by the majority of Blacks and Whites in Atlanta at that time who wanted to maintain things as they were. Some of our Black college presidents were more concerned about maintaining equanimity on their campuses than about promoting racial equality in their communities. Many of our Black college teachers (like the South Carolina public school teachers who had refused to support Septima Clark's and the NAACP's efforts to equalize their pay) were more worried about their jobs than about ending segregation in the South despite the protective covering of their private school status. And too many Black preachers acted as if the last pharaohs to get in the way of God's people lived in Egypt three thousand years ago. That's why I stopped going to church in the community during my senior year in college although I did continue to be nourished by chapel services at Spelman and Morehouse.

Some of my loneliest and most instructive moments occurred on May 16, 1960, when I stood with Lonnie King, Julian Bond, Johnny Parham, Ben Brown, and a few other key leaders of Atlanta's student movement on the lawn in front of Atlanta University's Trevor Arnett Library. We were waiting to see if any students would show up to march with us to the state Capitol. We had decided to conduct a march after the Ku Klux Klan had threatened to block any further demonstrations by Black students in the aftermath of the Appeal for Human Rights and the sit-ins that had stirred up Atlanta's racial pot.

The day before our planned march a few student leaders had met with our six college presidents. After the Appeal for Human Rights and sit-ins had occurred, we met regularly with them to discuss our ideas and general plans and to hear their concerns and advice. Atlanta Police Chief Jenkins, a decent man, joined us. He expressed his worry about threatened Klan violence and about ensuring our safety. When we students refused to back down, we, he, and our presidents worked through a planned route and reached what my peers and I thought was a balanced compromise between our free speech and assembly rights and those of the Klan. We agreed to be peaceful and disciplined in our actions so as not to provoke White violence but said we would not have Klan threats deter us. From our first involvement in civil rights demonstrations, thanks to Dr. King's teachings and example, we were prepared to accept but not inflict violence on others. When a young Black male attorney came to help me out in 1964 in Mississippi and tried to give me a gun to protect myself because I lived alone in Jackson I refused to touch it. My upbringing and the teachings of Dr. King made the thought of killing another abhorrent even for self-defense. When my husband and I visited Golda Meir in Jerusalem in 1968, I understood when she said, "We could forgive the Arabs for killing our sons but could never forgive them for making us kill their sons."

Each of the student leaders attending the meeting with our college presidents thought we had agreed upon a reasonable plan that we would share with our fellow students in chapel convocations on our respective campuses the next morning. I did so at Spelman and urged my Spelman sisters to join me and students from other colleges in front of Atlanta University's Trevor Arnett Library at the appointed hour to begin our march to the Capitol and then to Auburn Avenue's Wheat Street Baptist Church for a mass rally.

To my shock and dismay, Dr. Manley, Spelman's president, stood up after I sat down and urged Spelman students not to participate. He stressed all the dangers but none of the values at stake. As the few of us students gathered together at the assigned place and time, we learned that nearly all of the other college presidents had done as Dr. Manley did and discouraged students from joining our march. Clark College's president Dr. Brawley had gone so far as to lock the dormitories to try to make it impossible for students to leave the campus.

The moments felt like days as we huddled together and gazed on the empty lawn stretching before us. But then, after what seemed an eternity of waiting, we heard singing from a distance that got louder and louder as a line of Morris Brown students, whose campus was the farthest away, began to file onto the lawn in front of us. Like magic, other students began to pour out from their campuses from all directions. Some jumped out of their dormitory windows at Clark. Joyfully and purposefully, we marched singing, about one thousand strong, past the Klan hecklers with their hateful jeers and placards who were kept behind ropes and other street barriers manned by Police Chief Jenkins and his officers.

The tumultuous welcome from the packed crowd at Wheat Street church, the grinning welcoming committee of college presidents lined up across the stage, and the surprise entrance of Dr. King who'd flown up from Montgomery to encourage our youthful efforts taught me some lifelong lessons: hang on when life gets rough for pain and progress are Siamese twins just as midnight and dawn are regular hours in God's days.

From that day, I learned that risk and failure have few friends and victory many and that one should struggle to follow one's conscience whatever the consequences. I also remembered that one should not wait for others, especially those in power, to say it's all right to act when you know in your soul—after thinking through the pros and cons of doing something and doing nothing—that acting is right. My good friend Saul Alinsky once told me that the most immoral act of all is to do nothing in the face of injustice—a course so many choose most of their lives.

During the Easter weekend of 1960, I took my first plane ride, from Atlanta to Raleigh, North Carolina, on an airplane chartered by Dr. King's organization at Ella Baker's behest. Student leaders were traveling to Shaw University to share experiences and to see how we could sustain and strengthen our student movement challenging southern segregation. While some in the Southern Christian Leadership Conference (SCLC), the organization Dr. King now headed and that Ella Baker helped organize, sought to incorporate sit-in leaders as SCLC's youth arm, Ella Baker discouraged this course. She urged us to develop our own organization. The Student Nonviolent Coordinating

Committee (SNCC) was the eventual result of her urging. SNCC lasted six years sustained by the extraordinary organizing efforts in Mississippi led by the saintly and brilliant Bob Moses and in Alabama, Georgia, Tennessee, and elsewhere by gifted leaders like Diane Nash, John Lewis, Jim Forman, Charlie McLaurin, Stokely Carmichael, Ruby Doris Smith, Bernard Lafayette, Ivanhoe Donaldson, and Charlie Cobb. SNCC brought together freedom-hungry and fearless youth with energy and creativity and willingness to push the edges of the envelope. Ideas like the Mississippi Freedom Democratic Party's challenge to Mississippi's Jim Crow delegation at the 1964 Democratic Convention in Atlantic City and the Mississippi Freedom Summer project, which opened up the violent, unjust, closed Mississippi society to public view, came from SNCC's Bob Moses.

◆

Beginning in March 1960, my college diary reflects this time of powerful excitement and change.

MARCH 4, 1960

Now as never before is the chance offered to do something. This is a history-making epoch where we—me—the young—can be major characters. Now is the time to act—to work—to sacrifice.

Life is so pressing. Time is so strange. I'm very frantic in my quest to use it and not waste it. Each moment must be made to count.

I'm afraid and discouraged about my future yet feel a strong pull of destiny on the other. These are strange times and I'm torn apart.

So much has happened since I last wrote here. Posey Poole—a Dutch woman, student of Negro poetry, and former Nazi prisoner— knew Anne Frank and talked of her to us. She was tremendously moving. William Warfield came with his big voice and bigger heart.

We are all in the air about sit-down protests now. Am damned sick and tired of our inactivity. A group of us have been planning—led by Lonnie King, an able and sincere person who's backed by the Kings; Julian Bond, Morris Dillard, Amos Brown (bright young NAACPer), Melvin McCaw, and Ed Harper are our caucus. The college presidents have been a big hindrance and we are to meet with them tomorrow and discuss the issue. For the most part, they're a bunch of handkerchief heads—unworthy of respect and motivated by self-interest. When are we going to outgrow ourselves, God?

Last night at Howie's we were interviewed by an *Atlanta Journal* reporter. He is doing an article on Negro opinions. It was an interesting session: Julian Bond, Morris Dillard, Marjorie McClenden, and Johnny Popwell were there. Am afraid the article is going to have some repercussions because of our attack on Clements [President Rufus Clements of Atlanta University] and his damn conservatism. Couldn't care less.

Asked the reporter without forethought what would happen if I applied to Emory's law school. He thought it a great idea. God please show me what I am to do.

MARCH 5, 1960

Dr. Mays is so inspiring. He said: "Life is serious business—be high—noble—seeking. Every minute is an eternity—you must use it. There is much to do and so little time to do it. If you live to be ninety, life will still be all too short."

Today's meeting with the six college presidents and students lasted 4¹/₂ hours. A lot, I feel, was accomplished. The doubts and grievances I had were cleared up and I came out rather impressed with the idea of the Manifesto. Roz did a good job. [Roslyn Pope, my fellow Merrill Scholar and gifted pianist had drafted it.] We all corrected it by adding and subtracting certain things. In rough finished form it works well. They [the presidents] are not issuing the Manifesto as a final or last gesture and assure us that they're not trying to hinder us from whatever else we want to do—sit-downs, boycotts, talking to Governor Vandiver, or whatever.

It was a fascinating meeting for me because of the workings of the presidents together. President Clements is a smooth operator, suave, a real manipulator. Can't guess him. He's a patrician in the truest sense of the word. Dr. Richardson [president of Gammon Theological Seminary] was impressive—a thinker, sincere, and concerned with the students. I liked him. Dr. Manley [president of Spelman] without influence. Dr. Cunningham [president of Morris Brown] was distracted and distracting. Dr. Brawley [president of Clark College] absolutely silent—never opened his mouth, thank heavens. Dr. Mays is Dr. Mays. Amazed how Rufus Clements talks to him.

Other student groups went down to Rich's to get served at 6th floor restaurant. Am flabbergasted at Morris and Benedict College student protests. Know Dr. Bacote and Dr. Rubin [presidents of these colleges who were friends of my family] are stewing.

Help me to do the right thing and to be sincere and honest. Clean me of my underminings and make me fit for Thy service. We need Thee dear God and Thy loving guidance.

MARCH 9, 1960

The time has come for you, Marian, to have a frank talk with yourself. Where are you headed? You are in the midst of a history-making epoch. The Manifesto today is provoking all kinds of reactions and here you stand helpless. Get a hold of yourself and then forget yourself. What do you really want more than anything in life? I want to be good and a true feeler and doer of life.

MARCH 10, 1960

We are meeting our group again. The Manifesto came out. Good reactions. Some threats. Mayor Hartsfield met with student leaders yesterday. Nothing accomplished. Meet with 6 of 134 signers of pro-cause Ministers Manifesto tomorrow to discuss tactics—certainly a good sign.

I am to survey City Hall tomorrow. Am going to lead one of groups in our wildcat strike to be carried out the first of the week. Think it'll be effective.

Snow outside 3 or 4 inches deep. Is simply beautiful. No school held today. Thank God. Wish the same thing would happen Monday!

Bless my Mama. Read and righten our hearts.

MARCH 16, 1960:
SOMETHING WORTH LIVING AND DYING FOR!

Yesterday was a great experience. We carried off our "sit-in" strike demonstrations and have raised quite a bit of stir. About 200 of us took part and I will never forget the beautiful spirit manifested by every one of them. Before we left yesterday morning, we congregated in Dean Sage Hall [at Atlanta University] for final instructions and pep talks. Otis Moss got up and talked of the things we should be prepared for—abuse, hurt, and even death. We were all willing—some a little queasier than others. He then called several ministers from ITC [Interdenominational Theological Seminary] up front to lead us in several stanzas of "Amazing Grace." It was beautiful.

APRIL 10, 1960

Here it is nearly a month later and I've yet to write of all the events. It's impossible to recollect everything. Just heard Martin Luther King, Jr., speak for the first time—for our 79th Founders Day—and he was great! There's something almost holy about him—powerful—assured. He has found the meaning of life in God. Hope and pray by the time I'm 29 I will have done half so much for people and the world. He said, "Segregation's a cancer killing democracy's health. Segregation says God made a mistake in creating me a Black brother."

He talked about four mountains that had to be removed: (1) the mountain of moral and ethical relativism; (2) the mountain of practical materialism; (3) the mountain of racial segregation (Black supremacy as bad as White supremacy); and (4) the mountain of chronic disorder and violence. "We have been there in the mountains much too long. We must go from Egypt to Canaan." And he described three groups of people: (1) been down so long, down don't bother me. Will stay in Egypt rather than fight their way to the Promised Land; (2) half-way-outs—don't know whether to go back into Egypt or to go on to the Promised Land; and (3) Promised Land at any cost. He said to love all though you can't like everybody.

He also talked of three kinds of love: Eros, Platonic, and Agape. Used the language beautifully—a real power. His mother read the scripture. He ended by telling us, "If you cannot fly, run; if you cannot run, walk; if you cannot walk, crawl. But keep moving. Keep moving."

Sitting in my room listening to Brahms' violin concerto, again my mind goes to Martin Luther King and life. What people do with life—

how much some do and others how little. Thank God for a glimpse of beauty, a taste of life's savor. I must go back for more and more. I want to live. To live well, high, humble, loving, completely.

APRIL 28, 1960

To my dear God and life. If I lived to be a thousand years old, I could never be thankful enough for the great goodness given me, for many wonderful people have come into my life and touched me profoundly: Howard Zinn, Charles Merrill. I want to be great to say thank you to You and to them. Mr. Merrill and I had a 2½ hour talk Saturday and he offered me a job at his Commonwealth School in Boston whenever I wanted it. This morning beyond my wildest dreams came a letter from the John Hay Whitney Foundation saying I'd been granted a $1700.00 fellowship for graduate study next year. I don't know what to do. I'm so happy and grateful. I never expected to get it. Howie wants me to apply to Harvard. Help me God, to do what is right. Strengthen and direct me. Oh God—work through thy unworthy servant.

APRIL 29, 1960

Dear, dear God of my life. These are the most exciting, rewarding, and gratifying days of my life. Change is pervading—change I'm helping bring in. I'm useful and I'm serving and I'm so thankful.

Tonight I went over to the Congregational Church to hear Martin Luther King speak about weak decency. He was wonderful. He's almost Christ-like. Went up afterwards and he greeted me as if I were an old and dear friend. Has promised me a conference next week. Before the service began, I met Lillian Smith, author of *Strange Fruit*, and how accessible she was—so free and friendly. She graciously agreed to come over to Spelman and speak to my freshman study group.

Marvin Martin told me tonight—he's a Southern boy from Tennessee who's perfectly wonderful and is Arne's [my Norwegian exchange student friend] roomy—that Arne had repercussions from picketing last Saturday from the KKK and Georgia Tech officials. I love and respect him dearly. After the program, we all went to the Co Co Tree on Peachtree—a mixed bunch of 5 Negroes and about 8 Whites. . . .

Have decided to apply to Georgetown and get my masters and then go on to Harvard next year for my doctorate.

June [a White college student who grew up in Bennettsville] wrote the most wonderful editorial in the *Agnes Scott* paper about me and the racial situation after I spoke at Agnes Scott.

We grew up in the same small town but never met until after the sit-ins brought her White women students and my Black women students together in Atlanta. Things are moving all over. They [Agnes Scott] invited our exchange students over last night and more are making plans to come over and visit. There were many Agnes Scott girls to hear Dr. King tonight. Oh dear God—thank you for purpose and struggle. Make and keep us thy humble and dedicated servants.

Help us to become the best possible persons. Teach us to seek after truth relentlessly, and to yearn for the betterment of mankind by endless sacrifice. Help us to find life—to serve life—to *feel* life. To be alive and aware is my prayer. Help us to blossom and grow and to give absolutely. Make me steel-strong in my purpose and the best person I can be.

We are making history. We are taking upon ourselves the problems of the time and what a good burden. Help us to be worthy of our great call!

MAY 5, 1960
What a sweet, humble, and wonderful person Lillian Smith is! Went to party the Mike Goldbergers gave for her. She hugged me goodnight and said how beautiful she thought I was. I was overwhelmed. . . . She has cancer. She's very brave.

Went to see Martin Luther King, Jr., today but he was busy in press conference with African leader Kenneth Kaunda. Am to see him next Tuesday.

Let us be Thy humble servants.

A new South is being born with a new people. A new world is being made thanks to the Lillian Smiths and Martin Luther Kings.

MAY 17, 1960

Yesterday was a great day for the Negro people of Atlanta. We marched towards the Capitol (were detained by Police Chief Jenkins) and went on to Wheat Street. Were about 1000 of us. The meeting at Wheat Street was phenomenal and the spirit rejuvenating. Dr. Martin Luther King, Jr., came out of nowhere and the place went wild. Otis Moss gave a gem of an address. College presidents, who were against it but students did it despite their biddings, now greeted "their" students. Make us Thy humble servants. Use us.

MAY 19, 1960

Had the most fabulous afternoon with Dudley Doust from *Time*. They're doing a cover story on the sit-ins and they are interviewing students the South over. We talked for 7½ hours. Had dinner at Paschals.

◆

On this heady note the Atlanta portion of my diary ends. I spent a far less engaging summer as a switchboard operator in Arlington, Virginia, saving money for Yale where I'd been accepted and had decided to go for law school. I lived in Washington with my sister Olive and her family. It took many job interviews for a young Black college graduate to find work. An Arlington firm—Psychological Research Associates—finally hired me. One of the firm's principals, Dr. Paul Berry, was a Swarthmore graduate married to a fellow Swarthmore graduate, Sarita, who was Black. One of the firm's White secretaries, Carol, outraged at finding me at the switchboard and being asked to train me, overcame her initial racial anger and did so. She and I became fast friends and she later enrolled as the first full-time White student at Spelman College. I never knew of Carol's antipathy until she wrote about it in a paper for one of Howard Zinn's classes at Spelman.

⊹ 7 ⊱

THE YALE YEARS

William Sloane Coffin, Jr., Malcolm X, and Getting Ready for Mississippi

I WENT TO LAW SCHOOL because law was the tool I thought I needed to fight racial discrimination in the South in the early 1960s. Law school had never crossed my mind until one day during my senior year in college while I was doing volunteer work in the local NAACP office in Atlanta. After sorting all the requests for legal assistance from poor Black citizens who could not afford lawyers or who sought to challenge discriminatory practices, cases White lawyers would not touch, I wondered why in the world I was thinking about studying nineteenth-century Russian literature or going into the Foreign Service when the freedom and justice struggle was right here at home. It was time to jettison plans to live abroad and jump into the home fray for freedom.

My diary shows my mother was not excited about my decision to go to law school. There was no precedent in my family or community for such a choice. She did not know any Black women lawyers. I didn't either although I had heard of the formidable Constance Baker Motley who had worked with Thurgood Marshall at the NAACP Legal Defense Fund on many important civil rights cases. Connie later helped gain James Meredith's admission to "Ole Miss" and became the first Black woman federal district court judge. My mother wanted me to get a graduate degree (she was ahead of her time there) and, like many mothers, she wanted me to get a good job and a good husband. But as she always did, when she saw my mind was made up, she supported me. And she was proud of my being at Yale even if she did not fully understand why.

I wasn't sure how I would support myself through law school but took it one step at a time. The John Hay Whitney Fellowship, student loans, and jobs—and Yale chaplain William Sloane Coffin, Jr.'s generosity with free housing and food for a year—got me through. I had no idea how I was going to support myself afterwards or pay off my law school loans, but I knew I was going to Mississippi. Like my parents I had learned to live by faith and not just by sight.

The first day I walked into the dining room at Yale Law School in 1960 with my newly discovered group of Black women friends— Amelia Cobb in the drama school, Hildred Roach in the music school, Eleanor Holmes (now Norton) in the law school, and Ruby Puryear (now Hearn) in the biochemistry department—Black male students, shocked and delighted with the unexpected bounty of Black women students, appeared instantly out of the woodwork to greet us.

Ten women were in my law school class in 1960. From some of the comments I overheard about us you would have thought that a massive invasion of aliens had descended. Yale Law School dormitories were closed to women and constitutional law professor Fred Rodell still held some of his classes at Mory's on High Street which did not admit women. I lived my first and third years at Helen Hadley Hall on Temple Street which was the segregated dorm for female graduate and professional students. Women had not yet been admitted to Yale's undergraduate college.

I was elected to the Yale Corporation in 1971 as the first woman alumni trustee (Hanna Gray, former Yale provost and later president of the University of Chicago, was selected as a successor trustee the same year and Eleanor Holmes Norton and Ruby Hearn were elected alumni trustees in later years). I decided to join the Yale Club in New York City, which still had not opened its membership to women. It was quietly done.

I hated law school but I had a mission and Mississippi on my mind. Many of my college friends in SNCC and Bob Moses had gone to Mississippi to begin the arduous and dangerous task of voter registration. In that state there were about 900,000 Black citizens and only four Black lawyers. Three of them had not gone to law school but had studied on their own. The one who had attended law school did not take civil rights cases.

Depressed by my complete lack of interest in property and contracts and corporations and legal procedure courses and wondering what in the world I was doing in law school when my friends were out on the front lines in Mississippi, Georgia, and Alabama, I threw myself into the Northern Student Movement designed to support SNCC's work in the South. A Yale undergraduate named Peter Countryman was a key figure in this effort as was Al Lowenstein, who entered my life during the Yale Law School years.

I spent my first summer during law school in the Ivory Coast, West Africa with Operation Crossroads Africa. A forerunner of the Peace Corps, it had been founded by a charismatic Black pastor, Reverend James Robinson of the Church of the Master in New York City. He sought to build awareness and bridges between American and African youth. Before we left for Africa our group stopped in Washington, D.C. where we were housed at the College of Preachers at the Washington National Cathedral in the neighborhood where I now live. We went to the White House to hear and meet President John F. Kennedy. Unbeknownst to me until 1998, CDF's current board chair and Philadelphia School Superintendent David Hornbeck was in the same White House group and also participated in Crossroads that summer.

My Crossroads trip was made possible by a scholarship from St. Philip's Episcopal Church, Thurgood Marshall's church in Harlem. Its distinguished and kind rector, Dr. Moran Weston, had me speak to the congregation and has remained a life-long friend. He was a founder of Carver Federal Savings and Loan Bank in Harlem which my niece Deborah Wright now heads as president. My Crossroads group lived at and built a fence around a secondary school in Bouaké, the Ivory Coast's second-largest city. We also traveled to Ghana where we stayed at the University of Ghana, met students, and co-existed with what seemed to me legions of lizards everywhere. I learned to step over rather than flee them and to try to scare them to hide my fear since there was no escaping them.

My second year of law school was immensely lifted by living with

Yale's chaplain, Bill Coffin and his wife, Eva Rubinstein, and their three children: Amy, Alex, and David. I luxuriated hearing Eva's father Arthur Rubinstein play the piano downstairs as I lay upstairs in my bedroom. Bill Coffin, inspiring, outspoken, and eloquent, was mentor, friend, and billboard for faith in action. He cagily used me to integrate the all-White male usher board at Yale's Battell Chapel, calculating that some Yalies would be afraid to protest the revolutionary presence of a woman usher for fear of being perceived as anti-Black. When Freedom Riders seeking to end segregation in interstate transportation ran into violent resistance, he recruited friends from Yale to join with Wesleyan University faculty members John Maguire and David Swift to go South. I begged to go. Bill refused on grounds it was too dangerous for a woman and took a Black male Yale law student named George Smith instead. I still haven't forgiven him! But his commitment to racial justice and his later arrest with Dr. Benjamin Spock in opposition to the war in Vietnam made him a lifelong hero to me. On the weekend in July, 1968, when he married me and my husband in Virginia, he met with one of his defense lawyers, former U.S. Supreme Court Justice Arthur Goldberg, who spoke at our wedding and graciously held my flowers when my husband and I exchanged rings.

Bill Coffin's civil rights and Vietnam antiwar witness provoked much controversy at Yale but he never wavered. He later became senior pastor of the Riverside Church in New York City and then head of SANE—Committee for a Sane Nuclear Policy. A versatile and gifted musician who played his guitar and sang Russian songs at my wedding to my Russian-born mother-in-law's delight, a peerless preacher, a generous friend, and an exuberant and courageous bearer of God's word, I count him among the brightest lanterns during a dark era of national life.

◆

I visited Mississippi during one spring break in law school to remind myself why I was sitting in classes I found deadly dull and living in New Haven when my friends were organizing voters in the South. Medgar Evers picked me up at the airport, took me home to meet his wife Myrlie and their children, and then drove me up to Greenwood, Mississippi to join Bob Moses and others at the SNCC headquarters which was my destination.

Immediately upon our arrival in Greenwood we heard news of a drive-by shooting. The fear this provoked in the Black community and in me was palpable. Bob Moses and his SNCC colleagues knew they had to answer back by continuing to take people down to the courthouse to try to register to vote. I had promised my mother I would not get arrested and was warned by a Mississippi-born Yale law professor, Myres McDougal, that an arrest would surely keep me out of the Mississippi bar where I already faced high odds of exclusion. I approached the SNCC office the next morning determined to be helpful but to stay out of trouble.

As Bob, Jim Forman, and others persuaded some of the scared, raggedly clad but brave souls to walk in a line with them to the registrar's office, I found myself tagging along at the very tail end as a determined observer. That day was the first time police dogs were brought out to attack Black citizens attempting to register to vote. I watched in horror and shared the terror of the people who began to scatter and run as a German shepherd attacked Bob and ripped his pants. Bob did not flinch. I caught the car keys my SNCC friends threw me as they were being arrested and felt chilling isolation and fear watching local Mississippi law enforcement officials act ruthlessly and lawlessly. Helpless and outraged, I ran to a nearby phone booth and dialed John Doar in the Justice Department's civil rights division in Washington to tell him what was happening and to demand that FBI agents observing but doing nothing *do* something.

I remember his firm steely voice instructing me just to tell him the facts and to skip the emotion. I did but after I hung up shed furious tears of frustration as I wondered what to do next and whom else to call for immediate help. Jack Young, Jess Brown, and Carsie Hall, the three Black civil rights attorneys, were more than ninety miles away in Jackson. Huge numbers of Whites surrounded the courthouse where Moses and Forman and other SNCC workers had been taken to be tried immediately without a lawyer. The only person I recognized in the menacing crowd as I walked towards the front courthouse steps was Claude Sitton, the veteran *New York Times* reporter. He neither acknowledged me nor met my eyes. I knew then what it was like to be a poor Black person in Mississippi: alone. When I was blocked at the front courthouse door I attempted to enter by the side entrance but was again repelled by burly policemen. As I walked away through the milling mostly White male crowd and past the police cruisers with police dogs, I knew I would get through law school, however dull, would come back to Mississippi, and would walk into that and other courthouses to provide counsel to those unjustly treated.

MALCOLM X AT YALE

It was at Yale Law School that I met Malcolm X. I was sitting in the Law School auditorium reading and waiting for him to come on stage and speak. Although I was a Tolstoy, Gandhi, and King disciple, Malcolm X's sharp, sarcastic, funny, irreverent, tell-it-like-it-is rhetoric labeling Whites as devils who had oppressed Black America struck a resonant chord in my psyche. Experiences like the one I'd had in Mississippi were testimony to the evils of racial oppression he described. He provided a much needed outlet for the rage embedded in my and nearly every Black heart and soul in America. The Civil Rights Movement channeled much Black anger and rage into positive avenues. But Malcolm X knew how deeply White resistance and White privilege remained ingrained and how much needed to be done to free many Black minds enslaved by a sense of inferiority and many White minds enslaved by a sense of superiority instilled over nearly two centuries of slavery and segregation.

I was dumbstruck when I looked up from my reading and saw a tall, clean-cut, nattily dressed, freckle-faced man with glasses and neatly trimmed reddish hair smiling down at me, calling my name—"Miss Wright"—and introducing himself as Malcolm X. I was struck even dumber as he proceeded to tell me a number of facts about my life. I eventually recognized his source—a childhood friend in his entourage with shaved head, bow tie, and new last name of X, who was now a member of the Bridgeport mosque. I later renewed contact with another hometown friend who had become a Black Muslim when I went to New York to have several meals with Malcolm X in the Muslim's Harlem restaurant.

I was buoyed and enthralled by Malcolm X's intelligence, by his barbed humor (he chided me for ordering white bread during my first meal with him, saying it was utterly without nutritional value like White folks generally), and by his keen analysis of America's racial divide. But I was not recruitable. While many of his words resonated deep within me, made me laugh and clap and say "Amen" as much as they made many White people squirm, I was too deeply grounded in my Christian faith, unconvinced of the religious authenticity of the honorable Elijah Muhammad, unclear about the Black Muslim's true political agenda, and utterly unwilling to accede to their subservient role for women. I nevertheless felt enriched by the chance to cross paths and listen and converse and debate with this extraordinary man.

Like many I watched with deep interest Malcolm X's evolution, which included reaching out to Dr. King, and read with interest his words in *The Autobiography of Malcolm X* after he visited Mecca in 1964:

> During the past eleven days here in the Muslim world, I have eaten from the same plate, drunk from the same glass, and slept in the same bed (or on the same rug)—while praying to the *same God*—with fellow Muslims, whose eyes were the bluest of blue, whose hair was the blondest of blond, and whose skin was the whitest of white. And in the *words* and in the *actions* and in the *deeds* of the "white" Muslims, I felt the same sincerity that I felt among the black African Muslims of Nigeria, Sudan and Ghana.
>
> We were *truly* all the same (brothers)—because their belief in one God had removed the "white" from their *minds*, the "white" from their *behavior*, and the "white" from their *attitude*.
>
> I could see from this, that perhaps if white Americans could accept the Oneness of God, then perhaps, too, they could accept *in reality* the Oneness of Man—and cease to measure, and hinder, and harm others in terms of their "differences" in color.

His assassination in New York City in 1965 cut short the transformation of another hero who gave hope to Black children and to America. His wife and children who witnessed their husband's and father's killing carried on. Malcolm X's transformation to El-Hajj Malik El-Shabazz left all Americans much to think about if we are to grow beyond racism as he did.

GETTING READY FOR MISSISSIPPI

During my Yale years I shared a platform with Dr. King at Wesleyan University and in August of 1963 stood with uncontained excitement and tears with Bob Moses, Julian Bond, Ella Baker, and over two hundred thousand others as Dr. King told all America about his and our dream at the March on Washington. Renewed and buoyed by that gathering I headed north for my last year of intensive preparation to become a civil rights lawyer.

God was headed south to Mississippi and Alabama and Georgia and Louisiana and North Carolina and I went along for the scariest, most exhilarating, most challenging years any human being could hope for. On the way to Mississippi, though, I stopped for a year in New York City to place myself under the tutelage of an extraordinarily gifted and committed band of attorneys at the NAACP Legal Defense and Educational Fund, Inc. (LDF) headquartered then at 10 Columbus Circle.

Providentially LDF had created the Earl Warren Fellowship Program named after the great Chief Justice of the U.S. Supreme Court who had led the high court to unanimously decree public school segregation unconstitutional. The program began the year I graduated from law school to help young attorneys seeking to practice in the South. Julius Chambers and I were the first two Earl Warren Fellows. He was the first Black editor-in-chief of the Law Review at the University of North Carolina Law School, later succeeded Jack Greenberg as head of LDF, and is now chancellor of North Carolina Central University in Durham, North Carolina. We received a year's rigorous training at LDF's New York City headquarters under Jack Greenberg, James M. Nabrit, III, Constance Baker Motley, Derrick Bell, Norman

Amaker, Leroy Clarke, Mike Meltsner, and Frank Hefron. I learned an enormous amount about practical lawyering from these fine lawyers whose standards of excellence I have not seen bettered. We also were exposed to leading law professors and civil rights lions of the time and adopted into a network of LDF cooperating attorneys throughout the South and country who were litigating civil rights cases in their communities with LDF technical and financial assistance. These relationships nurtured Julius' and my confidence for the tough battles ahead and became a lifelong community of support and inspiration.

I learned more that year in LDF's practical school of lawyering about the real workings of the legal system than I had in the prior three years in law school. I also learned that the wheels of justice grind exceedingly slowly. One of my first assignments at LDF was to draft the brief for college students like myself who had been arrested for sitting in at lunch counters throughout the South. Some of these cases had wound their way on appeal up to the U.S. Supreme Court several years later. Their eventual successful resolution lifted the legal cloud hanging over my own head from my arrest on March 15, 1960 for sitting in at the City Hall Cafeteria in Atlanta for which courtly Donald Hollowell was my LDF cooperating attorney. I did not return to that cafeteria until 1988 when I visited Andy Young who was by then mayor of the city of Atlanta.

In the 1960s, there was a demonstrated need for more lawyers to do the trenchwork for civil rights. As moving and important as the Montgomery bus boycott was in emotionally galvanizing a city and a nation to end decades of segregated public buses, the ultimate victory was in the federal courts where such segregation was outlawed. At a time when many movement feet were getting tired after countless days of walking and hitching rides and young Dr. King was becoming discouraged and worn down by incessant White harassment including the bombing of his home and obscene phone threats, the role of lawyers was crucial to the movement's success.

I was proud to join LDF's ranks with its trailblazing legal legacy to serve as part of the backup legal machinery for those demonstrating in the streets. My Earl Warren Fellowship provided three years of declining support after the year in New York City. A full salary of $7200 for the first year enabled me to live comfortably in Jackson, Mississippi where I opened an office to handle the anticipated onslaught of cases from Mississippi's Freedom Summer of 1964. I opened up a satellite office in Memphis, Tennessee to service anticipated northern Mississippi cases in the law firm of civil rights attorneys Z. Alexander Looby and Russell Sugarman. Hundreds of White middle-class students soon brought visibility to the too long invisible struggles of local Black citizens for simple justice and the right to vote. I finally was going to witness on a sustained basis the unbelievably courageous efforts of Bob Moses and SNCC workers and local young people like June Johnson, Hollis Watkins, Willie Peacock, and Curtis Hayes to gain the vote; of courageous Black parents like Mae Bertha Carter and sisters Winson and Dovie Hudson and others who risked all to desegregate Mississippi public schools; of Fannie Lou Hamer who let her light shine everywhere she went; of Hartman Turnbow in Holmes County whose elocution of wisdom is not capturable on paper and who took no guff from anybody White or Black; of E. W. "Pops" Steptoe in fearsome Amite County whom I used to visit with Bob Moses; and of Amzie Moore—wise, warm, calm, helpful Amzie—who took youthful freedom fighters into his home and heart and showed us the rounds and rules for survival.

All of these great Black foot soldiers in the army of justice awaited me on arrival in Mississippi and sustained me all the while I lived there.

The White lawyers were not as welcoming.

8

THE MISSISSIPPI
YEARS

❦

WHEN I FIRST WALKED into federal court in Jackson, Mississippi in 1964, not a single one of the stony-faced White men sitting around the table would shake my hand as I went around the table to greet them in segregationist Federal District Judge Harold Cox's chambers. Their shock at my presence and the strained silence made me feel I'd stumbled into forbidden territory and a closed club. And I had. But I was uncertain whether it was my gender or race or the combination that struck these men speechless and immobile. Although Constance Baker Motley had blazed the way earlier, I never saw another local female attorney during my four years of practice in Mississippi.

Over the next months and years as the initial shock at my presence wore off some of these men tried to hold on to dying ideologies and modes of control and to fit me into a comfortable niche. I was surprised a few months after my chilly federal courthouse welcome to answer a knock on my front door one evening and to see an opposing prosecuting attorney grinning sheepishly, there to pay what he announced was a personal visit. He wrongly assumed that the sexual interest of an older, unattractive, married professional White opponent would be welcomed by a twenty-four-year-old Black female lawyer whose mind was stayed on freedom and justice and certainly not on adultery or him. He was not invited into my home. Other White lawyers, judges, and law enforcement officials attempted to separate me from my poor Black clients with "you and them" comments at counsel table. Still others pretended I simply did not exist which required regularly choreographed dances of combat. Grenada, Mississippi Sheriff Suggs Ingram would lock his jail doors if he saw me coming to visit or to get a client out of jail and let me ring and ring with his back turned to me through the glass front door. I'd have to resort to a telephone call to angrily insist I be allowed to enter and visit my clients.

Over time and after many trials before him federal Judge Harold Cox thawed a bit. However, I never forgave him for ordering Neshoba County Sheriff Rainey and Deputy Sheriff Cecil Price, convicted of conspiring to kill civil rights workers James Chaney, Andrew Goodman, and Michael Schwerner in the summer of 1964, to sit down next to me at my counsel table in his Meridian courtroom. I was there waiting to defend *Ebony* magazine against a libel charge brought by a young White Mississippian incorrectly identified in the magazine as having attended an interracial gathering. Perhaps Judge Cox thought he was chastening Rainey and Price by sitting them with me or simply did not think about how I would feel at all. I was outraged and felt ashamed of the hatred they provoked in me. I felt their evil well up in me and realized that I was capable of wanting to see them harmed. I profoundly oppose capital punishment not only because there is no definitive proof that it is a deterrent and because it has been disproportionately applied against Blacks and the poor and has taken the lives of innocent people, but because "vengeance is mine" saith the Lord. I was ashamed and scared of my vengeful spirit.

I'll never forget the day I visited a young Black death row client in a rural Georgia prison accused of killing a White farmer. Coming off the elevator I nearly bumped into the ugly white wooden electric chair never out of sight of those on death row awaiting final judgment. Hours later I was in the library of an Atlanta courthouse researching how many Blacks and Whites had been executed in Georgia's history when a loud, rude White man burst in grinning and shouting, "Hot damn, they got him." He was referring to the assassination of President John F. Kennedy in Dallas. I rushed with others to the nearest television set and could hardly get away quickly enough from the hateful glee of some of those surrounding me.

Being the first Black woman lawyer in Mississippi had its advantages as well as drawbacks. It allowed me to speak in tones to White sheriffs and policemen that most Black males never could have dared and gotten away with. My three brave brother attorneys—R. Jess Brown, Carsie Hall, and Jack Young—for years the only legal assistance available for Mississippi Black citizens seeking to challenge the status quo—tolerantly guided my fearless youthful steps. My admiration for their endurance and survival skills and commitment deepened as I pondered their years of chipping away at the walls of segregation without the glare of outside media or much compensation. They are among the many unsung heroes and heroines who sowed seeds of racial justice that led to gardens of righteous change all over our nation. Among the hundreds of cooperating civil rights attorneys melded together by the Legal Defense Fund to challenge segregation, Jess, Jack, Carsie, and Arkansas lawyer Wiley Branton, whose ancestors helped found Leflore County, Mississippi (the county seat of which is Greenwood), taught me how to survive and navigate the intricacies of Mississippi's feudal legal system which no textbook could teach and instructed me in the social etiquette of lawyering.

Mississippi had a long residency requirement (fifteen months) designed to keep "outsiders" like me from practicing in the state. You were automatically admitted to the Bar if you had attended the University of Mississippi ("Ole Miss") Law School. I technically served as Jess's, Jack's, and Carsie's law clerk in order not to be charged with illegally practicing law without a license while I fulfilled my residency. I did a huge amount of work aided by volunteer lawyers who visited during the hot summer of 1964 including Ed Koch and kind Harvard law professor Mark deWolfe Howe. Jess, Jack, and Carsie signed all the papers and appeared with me in court to introduce me as their colleague. Brilliant University of Pennsylvania law professor Tony Amsterdam (now at New York University Law School) would drive down to Mississippi, write a slew of briefs, give wise counsel about legal strategies, and drive back to Philadelphia.

After the residency period—and a three-day exam for which there was no course and in which one could be asked to state verbatim any statute among the many volumes of the Mississippi code—I did get into the Bar. Happily I had a secret angel in the form of one of Judge Cox's law clerks, Ed Wright, a Harvard Law School graduate who shared his notes and intelligence about the most frequently asked questions, issues, and statutes.

I began to understand on my first visit to Greenwood that I played a role beyond what I perceived. I did not realize how much I carried in my persona the dreams, expectations, and hopes of young and old Black citizens of Mississippi. I'll never forget the disappointed looks of those who heard there was a Black lady lawyer in town (I was actually only a law student) and who came to look for and at me. When they saw me in blue jeans and an old sweatshirt they were crestfallen. I never wore jeans in public again in Mississippi and made it a point to try to meet the expectations of poor Black Mississippians of how a proper lady lawyer should dress and act. I wanted them to be proud of me and cared enough about them to look my best, prepare my best, and fight for them as hard as I could.

Practicing law in Mississippi during the extraordinary years between 1964 and 1968 taught me about the enormously high costs of social change in violence, economic reprisals, harassment, fear, and lives lost.

I grew up next door to the Morris Funeral Home which I hated. I was traumatized at a very young age by a cruel older woman who pulled me inside the embalming room to view cadavers before they had been prepared for public viewing. The long-term nightmares this provoked were not repeated until a day in Jackson in 1964 when a sheet was pulled back in a mortuary revealing the body of a young Black man-child shot to death.

Slight of build, an innocent who had arrived in Jackson looking for work, the young man, around twenty, was walking down the street at the wrong time in the wrong skin and was picked up allegedly in a police dragnet hauling in Black males. He was jailed and allegedly slain in self-defense by a bullet at close range, by several White police officers in a tiny jail cell I later visited with disbelieving eyes, mind, and heart. They alleged he attacked them and could not be otherwise subdued although he was unarmed and outnumbered.

I had not expected this experience when asked by a local NAACP official if I would accompany the young dead man's parents to view him and take burial clothes. Outraged by the story I was told about the senseless snuffing out of this young life, I readily agreed to go, but assumed I would sit in the waiting room. There are times though when one cannot sit outside. How could I say to these trembling, shocked, scared poor parents or to that all-business mortician that I did not want to go further—that I was afraid?

I did not feel again the chill of unjust death I experienced that day until I visited Auschwitz about four years later with my husband. I could not stop shaking from the sense of stark cold evil as I stood before the mounds of eyeglasses and toys and hair that had once belonged to living sacred human beings including children.

In my early Mississippi lawyering days, it was not an unusual experience to visit jailed civil rights clients and to find them beaten or abused, or to hear bombs go off in Jackson. I never cranked up my car in the morning without leaving the driver's door open having been instructed that if a bomb had been planted you had a chance that way of being thrown from the car injured rather than killed. The occasional random bullet I realized had whizzed by into the wall I'd just passed was somehow reassuring and motivating rather than paralyzing—for me proof of a higher presence to which I could submit come what may. I remembered Miz Tee's "When it's your time, it's your time, when it's not, it's not."

I marveled at the courage of those who faced violence and threats every day. As if yesterday, I see Hosea Williams, a Vietnam veteran on Dr. King's staff, climbing atop a car in Grenada, Mississippi near nightfall when civil rights demonstrations had been met by a feverish pitch of White violence and resistance. I looked out at the White police mob on one side of the street and at the mob of White citizens on the other surrounding the Black demonstrators (I chose to stand closer to the citizen mob) while Hosea sang and made us sing away our fears with "This Little Light of Mine, I'm Gonna Let It Shine."

Lessons learned about not being paralyzed by fear or deterred by violence were not the only ones. Practicing law in Mississippi taught me the essential interplay between local empowerment strategies and

strong national legal frameworks which had to be well enforced to ensure equal opportunity in the face of entrenched, resistant state bureaucracies. It taught the inextricable nexus between race and poverty
and the limitations of political power without economic power. It
taught the importance of follow-through and tenacity. My job as a
lawyer could not end when I got a child into a "desegregated" school
if his or her parents' names were tacked up in flyers on the telephone
posts the next day and their houses were shot into, their jobs and
credit lost, their sharecropper shacks and food commodities taken
away from them, or their children suspended from or harassed in
school. These lessons led to the founding of the parent body of the
Children's Defense Fund.

But the biggest lessons I learned in Mississippi which I wish everyone could get as forcefully as I did were positive. They were about the
strength and resiliency of the human spirit and the ability of determined people to resist and overcome evil through personal and collective will. Never have I felt the company of such a great cloud of witnesses for divine and human justice willing to risk life and limb and
shelter so that their children could be free and better educated. I thank
God for Medgar Evers and Bob Moses and Fannie Lou Hamer and
Vernon Dahmer, for Mae Bertha Carter and Winson and Dovie Hud-
son, and Aaron Henry, Annie Devine, and Victoria Gray, Jake Ayers,
and a legion of others who put a bigger cause ahead of self.

Many of these brave souls have stayed the course through today,
seeing some of the fruits of their labors in their children and grandchildren. Unita Blackwell, a former sharecropper and Head Start
worker described later, is now serving her second stint as the mayor of
Mayersville, Mississippi. One of Mrs. Mae Bertha Carter's children, so
mercilessly harassed when she and her siblings entered the "White"
schools in Drew, later served on the Drew school board. Jack, Jess, and
Carsie would be so proud that there are now over three hundred Black
lawyers practicing in the state and that two of our young law clerks
from the 1960s, Reuben Anderson and Fred Banks, became Mississippi Supreme Court Justices. Medgar would cheer the justice that
Myrlie Evers and the Dahmer families finally squeezed from Missis-

sippi juries in his and Vernon Dahmer's murder cases. These long overdue downpayments on justice for two among many extraordinary leaders remind us that the arc of the universe does still bend toward justice however slowly.

Mississippi has many ugly patches still and much racism has resurged in the state. But progress is evident if far from complete. Many Blacks have been elected to the legislature since Bob Clark and I walked around the virulent segregationist Theodore Bilbo's statue as Bob took his seat as the first Black legislator since Reconstruction on January 3, 1968. Today Mississippi has the highest number of Black elected officials in the nation.

But that political representation has not translated into real economic power for a critical mass of Black citizens. Over 43 percent of Black children nationwide were poor when I left in 1968; today 36.8 percent still are. The rates are even higher in Mississippi. Welfare "reform" is turning back the clock for many with low wages, jobs without benefits, inadequate child care, health care, training, and transportation. Life for too many Mississippi children is a nightmare rather than the dream they deserve.

The Children's Defense Fund's current Mississippi office which also serves the southern region is battling these more intractable economic and social problems and working to rekindle the spirit of movement and to forge the collective will to carry forth the valiant struggle begun by those described in this book. Too many Mississippi children do not know about the sacrifices of these heroes and heroines. We must teach them and take them by the hands and train them to stand up for their own futures as young people did in the 1960s.

Sadly, children like those standing by the road in Marks, Mississippi in Roland L. Freeman's photograph in this book, as the mule train left for Washington to participate in Dr. King's campaign seeking to end poverty, are still standing there waiting for us to come again to see and help them.

9

MISSISSIPPI MENTORS

Bob Moses, Fannie Lou Hamer, Mae Bertha Carter, and Unita Blackwell

BOB MOSES

FOR ME AND MY GENERATION of young civil rights workers, Bob Moses was, after Dr. King, the most influential person in our movement lives. I and all of us would do anything for Bob and follow anywhere he led because we knew he would do anything for us and sacrifice all to win justice for the poor disenfranchised people of Mississippi.

A Harlem-born graduate of Hamilton College who had studied philosophy at Harvard, Bob Moses left a job teaching mathematics at the Horace Mann School in New York City to work for SNCC. He had set up a voter registration project in 1961 in Mississippi which had the lowest Black voter registration of any southern state.

His unshakable calm, quiet leadership style, unquestionable integrity, and incredible courage and perseverance in the face of grave dangers inspired us again and again. He encouraged us to tap wellsprings of inner strength and possibility we did not know we had and helped us be so much better and braver than we realized we could be. He led by example and was prepared to give absolutely everything he had to the freedom struggle including his life.

I was not afraid when I was with Bob even when crouched on the floorboard of the car's backseat as we passed through McComb on the way to then notorious Amite County to visit E. W. "Pops" Steptoe's family. Louis Allen had been killed in broad daylight in Amite County because he had witnessed the murder of Herbert Lee who had tried to register to vote. Allen told federal officials he was willing to name the White killer if given protection. He wasn't. In January 1963 he was killed the day before he was planning to leave Amite County.

Bob did not let a split-open head wound keep him from walking into the registrar's office in McComb with his scared fellow citizens, determined to show local officials and his White assailants that violence would not turn him or the movement around. He knew he had to break the paralysis of fear among would-be voters and let Mississippi know he would not turn back until Black citizens could vote.

As patient as Job and determined to keep hope alive among his fractious and often unpaid band of SNCC workers, his quiet but steely will kept them and me carrying on and pushing on the heavy door to open Mississippi's closed society. He knew how hard and how important it was and how much time it would take to build the trust of local citizens who too seldom had seen leaders who stuck by them when times got really rough.

He devised the 1964 Mississippi Freedom Summer and with Al Lowenstein's assistance recruited hundreds of idealistic White college students to come into the state to bring visibility to the constant denial of human and civil rights of Mississippi Black citizens. Sadly, only when middle-class and privileged Whites feel threatened does a movement reach critical mass and attract enough media attention to mobilize public opinion.

I saw and shared his wrenching soul-searching at Western College for Women in Oxford, Ohio when the horrible news of James Chaney's, Andrew Goodman's, and Mickey Schwerner's disappearance swept through training sessions designed to prepare the White college students for Mississippi's realities. I saw this leader shoulder the burden of life and death consequences not just for himself but at that moment for so many others. I felt him struggle to determine what price others could be asked to pay to uphold one's ideals.

I bristle when I hear careless know-nothing media and political pundits and self-righteous ideologues excoriate the Sixties as a time of undisciplined behavior. Not my Sixties. Not Bob Moses' Sixties. Not

Mrs. Hamer's or Mrs. Viola Liuzzo's or James Reeb's Sixties. Not the Sixties of little Ruby Bridges, or the Jackson, Mississippi children loaded into cattle trailers and detained in the Jackson stockyards, or the Birmingham children knocked off their feet by powerful police fire hoses who went off to jail singing for their freedom. Not the Sixties of the four small girls blown asunder by a hater's bomb while attending Sunday school at the 16th Avenue Baptist Church in Birmingham.

Bob Moses led us through the very difficult Mississippi Freedom Summer and through a mock election in which 80,000 Black citizens showed they wanted the right to vote denied them by Mississippi's Jim Crow Democratic Party. He led us to Atlantic City where the Mississippi Freedom Democratic Party (MFDP) with Joe Rauh as counsel unsuccessfully sought to persuade the Credentials Committee at the Democratic National Convention to unseat the racist Mississippi Party regulars. Being right was not enough to overcome the might of the Johnson-Humphrey and establishment forces who expected MFDP to be happy with a symbolic compromise offering two seats rather than fair representation.

Bob Moses, human and not saint after all, was worn out from the cumulative struggles to register Black voters and the White violence it provoked, by the MFDP defeat in Atlantic City, and by the willingness of civil rights allies to compromise on what he, Mrs. Hamer, and the majority of the "unsophisticated" MFDP delegation thought was a matter of principle and right.

I watched with profound sadness and understanding this wonderful man leave Mississippi burnt out and temporarily disillusioned about interracial coalition building. I saw him for the last time for many years in Steven's Kitchen, our civil rights gathering place for breakfast, lunch, and dinner next door to my shabby Farish Street law office in Jackson above the pool hall. I was sitting at a table with our mutual White friend John Mudd who later headed the Child Development Group of Mississippi (CDGM), one of the largest Head Start programs in the nation. Bob would not sit down with us but beckoned me to join him at a different table. He had become convinced for the time being that Whites were a destructive force in the movement and that we Blacks had to rely only on our own strengths and efforts. While White students and others brought much needed political and media attention to the struggles of Mississippi Blacks, some Whites, so used to unquestioned leadership and control, found it hard to share power or to defer to Blacks even on their home turf. Bob had come to feel that the costs of White participation overrode the benefits. He did not like the Child Development Group of Mississippi (for which I served as a board member and counsel) taking federal Head Start dollars because he believed this would undermine the independence and self-reliance of local people. But children had to learn and hope had to stay alive.

Soon afterwards my deeply loved and admired friend went off to Tanzania via Canada to regroup, renew, and wait out the Vietnam War. He eventually returned home, resumed his philosophy studies at Harvard, and founded the important Algebra Project to help Black and poor children get onto the college track. His oldest daughter Maisha, a teacher in the Algebra Project, and my oldest son Josh, also a teacher, graduated from Harvard together.

Mrs. Fannie Lou Hamer

In 1977, on a flight to Hanoi with President Carter's delegation on the Missing in Action (the Woodcock Commission), I received a wire that Mrs. Fannie Lou Hamer had died. I mourned at the American ambassador's home in Vietiane, Laos by singing and playing some of the songs she had sung to keep the light of freedom alive during the dog days of civil rights struggle in Mississippi. A mighty lantern's flame had been snuffed out.

Mrs. Hamer's extraordinary life and courageous witness and words have been shared by many co-workers who were with her during countless tumultuous days of struggle. Kay Mills' fine book *This Little Light of Mine* chronicles her life and Charles Marsh's book *God's Long Summer: Stories of Faith and Civil Rights* devotes a chapter to her living theology. Stories by her friends Unita Blackwell, Mrs. Mae Bertha Carter, and other co-workers and my own moving encounters with her keep her spirit alive for me.

Mills tells the story of Mrs. Hamer, the twentieth child born of poor Mississippi sharecroppers, once asking her mother why they weren't White. She internalized and lived her mother's answer: "You must respect yourself as a little child, a little Black child. And as you grow older, respect yourself as a Black woman. Then one day, other people will respect you." And we did respect Mrs. Fannie Lou Hamer as a Black woman. And we loved her. I loved her.

I respected and loved her for her courage right after a cruel beating in the Winona, Mississippi jail. In Charles Marsh's moving account she describes being beaten "with a thick leather thing that was wide. And it had sumpin' in it heavy. I don't know what that was, rocks or lead. But everywhere they hit me, I got just as hard, and I put my hands behind my back, and they beat me in my hands 'til my hands . . . was as navy blue as anything you ever seen." The blackjack was passed to the second inmate who would be forced to beat a fellow prisoner. "That's when I started screaming and working my feet 'cause I couldn't help it." This enraged her White jailers who "just started hittin' on the back of my head." Although the beating left her flesh injured, one of her kidneys permanently damaged, and a blood clot over her left eye that threatened her vision, back in her "death cell" in that Winona jail hurting all over she found her voice which broke free as she sang:

> Paul and Silas was bound in jail, let my people go.
> Had no money for to go their bail, let my people go.
> Paul and Silas began to shout, let my people go.
> Jail door open and they walked out, let my people go.

Fifteen-year-old June Johnson from Greenwood, Mississippi and other SNCC workers including Annelle Ponder, Euvester Simpson, and Lawrence Guyot, some beaten and all scared nearly to death in their jail cells, heard Mrs. Hamer singing and began to sing too.

I respected and loved her for her wit that used to make us double over with laughter as she used it to teach us serious lessons about tolerance and decency towards the very Whites who oppressed her when she sought the vote for Blacks and the poor.

I respected and loved her for faithful practice of the hard message of Christianity which kept us from hating when we wanted to hate: "Baby you have to love 'em [White people] because they are weak." Or "It wouldn't solve any problem for me to hate Whites just because they hate me. Oh, there's so much hate, only God has kept the Negro sane."

I respected and loved her for scolding and seeking to redeem her White oppressors. Mrs. Hamer reached out to the wife of the Winona jailer whose husband had mistreated her and gently suggested she read several Bible passages including "[God] made of one blood all nations of men for to dwell on all the face of the earth." In court Mrs. Hamer asked the jailer who'd unjustly detained and ordered her beaten, "Do you people ever think or wonder how you'll feel when the time comes you'll have to meet God?" Mrs. Hamer said: "I hit them with the truth and it hurt them."

She hit timid Black leaders, especially preachers, with her truth when they were afraid to put their faith in action. Marsh quotes her saying: "It's all too easy to say sure, I'm a Christian, and to talk a big game. But if you are not putting that claim to the test, where the rubber meets the road, then it's high time to stop talking about being a Christian. You can pray until you faint . . . but if you're not gonna get up and do something, God is not gonna put it in your lap." She excoriated "chicken-eatin'" Black preachers who sold out to the White power structure and who would not support the movement.

She hit the SNCC workers with her truth when they resisted White involvement in the Mississippi summer Freedom Schools: "If we're trying to break down this barrier of segregation, we can't segregate ourselves."

And she hit Hubert Humphrey, ordered by President Lyndon Johnson to stop "that illiterate woman" and the Mississippi Freedom Democratic Party's 1964 challenge to the discriminatory Mississippi Democratic Party, with her truth after he urged her to accept an unjust compromise: "Do you mean to tell me that your position is more important to you than 400,000 Black people's lives?"

A bitter split developed in Atlantic City between Dr. King, Andy Young, the NAACP's Aaron Henry, and other of the more pragmatic leaders and Bob Moses, Mrs. Hamer, and the majority of MFDP delegates. The former were more open to accepting the largely symbolic offer made by President Lyndon Johnson's point persons including Senator Humphrey and his lieutenant Walter Mondale, who were eager to ensure Humphrey's place on the Democratic ticket as vice president and to keep powerful southern delegates from abandoning the party. Bob Moses and Mrs. Hamer, the majority of the MFDP delegates, and I opposed the compromise. Mrs. Hamer was not a practical politician accustomed to engaging in political dynamics where righteous public posturing and less righteous back-door negotiations went hand in hand. SNCC workers and unlettered but not unwise Black Mississippi citizens were relative novices at this brand of politics from which they had been largely excluded by Mississippi's closed politics.

Mrs. Hamer and her MFDP followers were less interested in being politically correct than in being morally correct as her dialogue with Unita Blackwell below shows. She wanted to sit at the Democratic Party table and not be thrown a few Democratic Party crumbs over the side. Her disbelieving question to Hubert Humphrey showed her unwillingness to play the politicians' game. I sometimes wonder whether the bedrock values, mother wit, and faith-driven courage of Mrs. Hamer and women like her might have prevented some American White males' catastrophic decisions that cost tens of thousands of lives. I love to imagine Mrs. Hamer sitting at the table with Robert McNamara and Henry Kissinger during discussions about the Vietnam War asking loudly and insistently, "Is this right? Would God like it?"

•

Mrs. Hamer came by her early political education the long and hard way. She was forty-four and working on a plantation when civil rights workers arrived in Sunflower County. From time to time, Mrs. Hamer came to hear them when they spoke about voter registration and raised her hand when they asked who would try to register to vote.

Soon afterwards she led a group of volunteers from a bus into the circuit clerk's office. The clerk told all but two to leave and only Mrs. Hamer was allowed to stay for the voter test. When she failed to interpret a section of the state constitution she was unable to register ("When I heard this story, it was the first time I realized Mississippi had a constitution!" she said). The police arrested and fined the bus driver (allegedly because the bus was "too yellow"). When the people who had come with Mrs. Hamer became frightened, she started singing and they scrambled together enough money to pay the fine so the bus driver could take them home. When Mrs. Hamer arrived home her plantation owner told her that if she wanted to stay she shouldn't try to register to vote. She answered him with her truth: "I didn't go down there to register for you. I went down to register for myself." He told her to pack her things and the children's things and he'd take them into town because she couldn't live there any more. When he relented the next day she refused his offer to allow her to return. Fearing for her safety, her husband "Pap" took her to live with relatives in another county. But she didn't stay there. Returning to town she said, "Well, killing or no killing, I'm going to stick with civil rights," and continued to attend voter registration classes and to speak everywhere. She was a wonderful speaker who let nothing turn her back although as she once said, "I'm never sure anymore when I leave home whether I'll get back or not. Sometimes it seem like to tell the truth is to run the risk of being killed. But if I fall, I'll fall five feet four inches forward in the fight for freedom. I'm not backing off."

On September 10, 1962, the day the Supreme Court ordered the University of Mississippi to admit Black student James Meredith, shots were fired into several homes of civil rights workers and local people active in the voter registration drive including the house where Mrs. Hamer was staying.

Mrs. Hamer weathered repeated violence and harassment. She received a $9,000 water bill from her county although her house lacked running water. She tried to register to vote again after she learned how to interpret the Mississippi constitution from citizenship classes only to be told she could not vote because she had not paid poll taxes for two years (how could she without being able to register?). But nothing dampened her spirits and she finally registered to vote and went on to teach others how to do so.

She later ran for Congress against segregationist Jamie Whitten, the powerful chair of the House Agriculture Committee who worked hard to keep Mississippi Blacks hungry and voteless. She fought until she died for good Head Start programs and to bring economic development to Mississippi through pig farming to help stave off the hunger of discarded sharecroppers. She was a delegate to the 1970 Democratic Party and ran for state senate and lost in 1971.

She gave everything for Jesus, freedom, and justice. I was so proud when she came to visit me in Washington to participate in the dedication of my first child Joshua Robert to God. May her spirit of grit, love, and courage infuse his life and all my and our children's lives.

I still try to be half as strong and half as good as Mrs. Hamer. It is my dream that the mothers and grandmothers of America will come together in our time across race, class, and faith and tell all those in power with our voices, votes, and organizing to let our children go from the bondage of gun violence that kills them every two hours; from the bondage of poverty and poor education that tracks them to prison rather than to college; from the bondage of drugs that comes from idleness, too few legal jobs, and too little purposeful service; and from the bondage of self-serving community and political leaders who have forgotten if they ever knew that the purpose of life and public office is not themselves but justice and service to the common good.

I was sitting in Jackson with a Mississippi college president's wife looking at television during President Johnson's inauguration. The president's wife glimpsed Mrs. Hamer at one of the inaugural balls and burst out, "Oh my goodness, there Mrs. Hamer is and she doesn't even have on a long gown." I replied, "That's all right, she's there and you and I with our long gowns are not."

So many Americans who are busy dressing up in fancy clothes don't stop to think about whether they are going any place in them that is worthwhile. Mrs. Hamer never made that mistake.

MRS. MAE BERTHA CARTER

It is impossible to overstate the amount of courage it took for Mrs. Mae Bertha Carter, her husband Matthew, and eight of their thirteen children to exercise their "freedom of choice" in 1965 to become the first and for several years the only Black students to attend formerly White public schools in Drew, Sunflower County, Mississippi. Sunflower was segregationist Senator James O. Eastland's home county. It was a scary, violent county during the height of the Civil Rights Movement. I always tried to leave it before sundown.

But the Carters didn't leave. They stayed, fought, and changed it as Mrs. Hamer did. They loved their children, wanted the best for them, and believed education was the ticket to freedom. They were determined to pay whatever it cost to get their youngest children out of the cotton fields. And they paid a lot.

I was privileged to be the Carters' lawyer when they sued in 1967 to challenge Mississippi's "freedom of choice" plan designed to avoid real desegregation. In the suit filed for Mrs. Carter and her children Larry, Stanley, Gloria, Pearl, Deborah, Beverly, and Carl in the U.S. District Court against the Drew Municipal Separate School District, I wrote: "Fear of White retaliation, firmly grounded in fact, has deterred other Negroes from choosing the formerly White school pursuant to the District's freedom of choice plan." I sought injunctive relief against the segregated and discriminatory system that placed a "cruel and intolerable burden" upon Black parents and children. We won the court decision throwing out Mississippi's so-called freedom of choice plan. But Mrs. Mae Bertha Carter and her children faced many tough daily battles ahead.

After she and Mr. Carter refused to withdraw their freedom of choice papers their plantation boss evicted them. But they were determined that their younger children would not have to share their older children's back-breaking days picking cotton and attending poor all-Black schools which operated only part of the school year and provided hand-me-down old White school buses and precious few books and supplies. "In that Black school, they had you paying for everything," Mrs. Carter told CDF staff in an interview a few weeks before her death. Wanting their younger children to attend better schools, the Carters stood united because "We thought it would later on make the world a better place. We knew it was the right thing to do." The older children signed their own freedom of choice papers and Mrs. Carter signed for the younger ones. "Don't care where you go in this world, you need an education. I don't know why, but I just knew it."

Their sacrifices were greater than most people would or could bear. The Carter home was shot into and fear of night snipers caused the family to sleep on the floor for several years. The land they had tilled for years was lost, their remaining crop was plowed under, credit was denied them, and they couldn't find any work or housing. In her marvelous account of the Carters' struggle, *Silver Rights*, Connie Curry details the cruelty White adults taught White children to perpetrate against the Carter children including urging them not to sit next to them in school and to call them names.

In a four-and-one-half-hour interview in April 1999, Miz Mae Bertha described how she felt as a mother when she first put her children on the school bus to go to the White school:

> I don't know. It feel so bad. But it was something that we had to do. We got up early in the morning, children got ready to go to school and we could look down the road and we could see the bus coming. We didn't have to wonder what bus it was. Because it was a bright, real yellow bus and we knew that was the White bus. Because they had been riding on these old broke-down piece of buses. So you just knew what was coming.
>
> And I stand on the porch until the children came out, got on the bus and the bus pulled off. And when the bus pull off, I went inside, fell down cross the bed and began to pray. I didn't say too much but Lord, take care of my kids.
>
> And when they come from school, I would go back on that porch and I see them about a mile away. And they get off the bus and I count them, one by one. Then I thank God. Lord I thank you for taking care of my children today.

And then I will ask them how was the day. And they began to tell me the things that happened at school that day. And then sometimes we sing.

And we—we couldn't forget, so we'll sing that song, [singing] "got up this morning with my mind, stayed on freedom, oh, I got up this morning with my mind, stayed on freedom, hallelu ... hallelu ... lujah." There's one thing they say, [singing] "Ain't no harm to keep your mind, stayed on freedom, it ain't no harm to keep your mind, stayed on freedom, hallelu,hallelu,hallelujah." And we would sing different songs, "Ain't Going to Let Nobody Turn Us Around," "Keep On Walking to Freedom Land." And then we'd feel better. And get up the next morning and go to school.

The Carter family stuck it out. The younger Carter children graduated from Drew public schools and seven of them went on to graduate from the University of Mississippi. One of them, Beverly, served on the Drew School Board. Two sons served in the Air Force for over twenty years, another son is a hospital administrator, and two daughters have management jobs.

Their mother was always there for them, listening and helping them talk it out. The only things she wouldn't let them say were that they hated all Whites or that they wished they'd never been born. Asked in April 1999 if she regretted sending her children to experience such relentless White hostility she answered:

No, unh-unh, not a one, no. I told the children anytime that I can stay at home and know my child is in Vietnam in that war still, he didn't know how he got there and why he was there. Two of them went. And going to Drew public school, he know he was trying to get a better education for himself and we knew it.

So, I always said, if you are going to die for something you should know what you are dying for. And he was—they was going to be dying for education. Over there, they didn't know what they were going to be dying for. But they had to go.

So, I didn't have no regret, because I know and my husband know there's nothing you can do in the United States without a education. You already dead. You got to face the fact, already dead. You just like fish out of the water. How long can that fish live out that water? You got to have some kind of skill. Don't fool yourself.

And now it's safe enough—they try to keep them out of these schools, they shot at us, they did everything to us. And, now, they get ready for a job—just a job—you can't get it.

Asked what was her best moment: "I tell you the best moment with me. When they all graduated from college and went on towards getting some jobs. That's my best moment. That's the best moment that I had. You can now go get you a job. And go in business if you want to."

Asked about the secret of her success in raising her children, Mrs. Carter said: "We didn't have a secret. We showed them love. They could come and tell us anything. My husband always quoted this to his children. 'When you're happy, I am happy. When you're sad, I'm sad.' He loved his children. They were our first priority. You can't forget about your children. Don't ever get too busy to listen to your children."

Mayor Unita

Unita Blackwell was the first Black woman mayor in Mississippi. Elected in the town of Mayersville, Mississippi, in Issaquena County in 1976, she served for nineteen years during her first stint and worked her way up to chair the Black Women Mayors' Caucus and to become President of the National Conference of Black Mayors in 1989. After she left office the first time (she is again Mayor), she was a MacArthur Foundation Prize Fellow. But she earned her late life honors the hard way and speaks movingly of experiencing "emotional violence every day" for her movement work in Mississippi. As Unita puts it, she "filed a lawsuit against almost every agency and operation of White people in the State of Mississippi." I was fortunate to serve as her lawyer for some of them. During one period, Unita says she got arrested every day for thirty straight days and was jailed about seventy-five times for trying to organize people to register to vote. After 1964 when she joined the movement, she says she never slept uninterrupted for years because she and her family and friends would take turns sleeping and mounting guard against the Klan. She shared with my son Jonah how it felt when a cross was burned in front of her house and she showed him the exact spot.

I recently persuaded Unita to tell her story for an oral history video with an audience of college students who crowded into the Shirley Comer Room at the former Alex Haley Farm, the Children's Defense Fund's center for spiritual renewal and intergenerational leadership development. They were rapt as she shared her life history and illustrated how she and her dear friend Mrs. Fannie Lou Hamer with whom she often shared a bed or floor had snoring contests. She claimed Mrs. Hamer always won!

As you will see from her words below, Unita has never stopped growing, learning, rolling with the punches, and punching back when she had to. She is always laughing and making other people laugh. Her creativity of expression is sometimes unrestrained by the niceties of grammatical syntax. This disturbed a bright student leader at Spelman who hailed from Mississippi and who knew that Unita and I were friends. She was, she said, confused about what to think of Mrs. Blackwell because she didn't speak "good" English. I told the student to listen to the substance and ignore the style because Unita had more to say worth listening to than thousands of proper-speaking saynothings. Unita warned her young charges at Haley: "Now you going to hear a lot of broken English and stuff here and if you all know better just put it back together and we go on. I know you can find them somewhere, the verbs and the adverbs and so forth." But I'll let Unita tell her own story and you listen in.

As a young girl I learned to be strong. I'd walk with my mother on hot days with the dust between my toes and want Mama to carry me, but she would say, "Come on, you can make it." I was raised up that way, my mother encouraging me saying, "You can make it." My mother couldn't read and write. My grandmother could. My grandmother was taught to read and write by her boss's wife, not because they were so gracious but because she was a cook and the woman wanted to have her recipes.

I grew up on a plantation in Mississippi and every summer me and my sister went to my aunt's in Arkansas to help out because she was sick. She *was* sick but that wasn't the reason. My mother sent us there until school started again to get us out of working on the plantation.

My father and uncle and our families had to move to Tennessee because the boss who was short got into an argument with my father who was very tall. The boss swung at my father and my father lifted him up by the collar. At that time you did not put your hands on White people. A Black man could be killed for that. So the family moved to Tennessee.

My childhood was one of ironing and washing and chopping and picking cotton but I loved books and had good teachers in school. Miss Franklin was particularly good to me and encouraged me to speak publicly in school. She told me that I was a good speaker, and that it was important to be the best you can be. She would make me speak every Friday and tell me how to stand, say your speech and smile. It was Miss Franklin who named me. The tradition in my family was for the oldest brother in the family to name the family's children so my uncle named me. But he could not read and write so he called the children by two initials. I was UZ. Miss Franklin told me I couldn't go through life like that so she named me Unita Zelma. I told my mother who thought it was a good idea. Teachers are so important to children. They are the next thing to parents.

When I was young I had a Black boyfriend but he was very light-skinned and I was very dark. He had a hard time with other children because he liked someone so dark and others were jealous because I had a light-skinned boyfriend. One time I went to "White town" to pick up the mail and a White boy called me "nigger, nigger, nigger." And we just got into it. When I got home and told my mother, she just took me and hugged me and said, "Don't worry about it. You're my child. You're my child." (Sorry to be crying. I could feel that. I'm sorry.) I saw fear in her eyes because she didn't know whether her whole family would be wiped out. That's the way it used to be. And we need that kind of love. My mother was ready to die for her child. From then I went on to understand this vicious race problem in this country and how color was so important even in our own race. And my friends was all kinds of colors. We were brown-skinned, light-skinned. But they said: "If you're light, you're all right. And if you're Brown, stick around. If you're Black, stand way back." So you know where I was supposed to stand.

I got teased by other children for being so Black, and I asked my mother why I was very Black and she replied, "Don't worry about it, you're honest." I hung on to that though I didn't really understand how it related. Children hang on to things adults say, and it's so important to be wise in what you say to children. When people criticized my color, I'd say, "Don't worry about it, I'm honest." I was determined to be whoever I was, I guess. They say my self-esteem was hanging on a thread but mother kept it going.

When my husband's grandmother died, we went to take over her land in Mississippi. I was worrying about how to educate my child and didn't want him working in the fields. It was the time of the so-called freedom riders and Stokely Carmichael showed up in my life and Charlie Cobb and they was out there in the fields with the overalls on. I'll never forget Stokely. He was really trying to get down with it so he could be like a farmhand. They came to the fields to talk to the people. But I knew they weren't locals because they were walking fast. No one walked fast in the Mississippi heat. Then they said, "Hello." The locals said, "How y'all feeling." And we say to each other, "That's them." I was leading Sunday school and two of the freedom riders came to my class. They didn't have on church clothes. We had a thing about church clothes. I told the class, "God helps those who help themselves," as Charlie and Stokely stood up and asked if they could speak. One was from Brooklyn and they couldn't understand his accent, but the other was from Virginia and they understood him. I asked them to come back to the 11:00 service to speak. They asked at the service if they could have a meeting in the church, and the parishioners voted that they could though there were some who opposed. The head deacon didn't approve so he said the sheriff said they couldn't have a meeting in the church. I called the sheriff on the phone to ask him about it and he said he hadn't said that and he'd sue whoever said he did. That was the first time I heard you could sue people like that [laughter]. I went back and told the people it was okay to have the meeting.

At the meeting I was encouraged to register to vote. I thought that was a good idea. I've been asked what made me get into the movement. It was the needs: the needs to be met for education, for us to live and eat and be decent and have the necessities of things in life. I stood up when they asked who would try to register. My husband pulled my dress to make me sit down and said, "Don't get up 'til I get up." I sat down and waited, and he didn't get up, so I poked him until he did stand, and then when he got up, I stood up, and I've been up ever since.

A group of us went to try to register, including several schoolteachers. Then trucks came with guns and circled the courthouse. The sheriff came and told us to stay away from the men who had encouraged us to register, that they were just outside agitators and "You all is good people. I been knowing you all these years." A woman from the group said, "Yes sir, you have, but I have this right." The sheriff got very red in the face, and it was awful to see the hate in the eyes of the White men who had come with guns. That's the day I got angry . . . I thought nothing from nothing leaves nothing and we have nothing, and we're going to have to stand for something. I was afraid, but that was the day I decided I was going to die for my freedom. I went in and began to convince others to go. We lost our jobs. I never did have a job from that day [working for] White people. So I became an "instant organizer" and got to know others who were working for freedom.

Unita told the listening young people about those who would come to civil rights meetings and then divulge the plans to the White police. She recounted a time when they were planning a demonstration the next day at a school and a woman who had been in their meeting left early. "I thought she was a Tom and suggested we change the plan. We did, and saw the next day that the police and the dogs were lined up at the school waiting for us." She also told about how she had four telephones in her house. When someone fired shots through the window, first you hit the floor, then you called SNCC in Atlanta, then the FBI, then the local police. She said she called the FBI once and told them there was a cross burning in the front yard. When the FBI asked how tall the cross was, "Obviously, I wasn't going to get off the floor to look out and see how tall the cross was." The FBI told her to preserve the cross in a gunny sack because they couldn't get up there right away. "*Mississippi Burning* was a lie," Unita asserted: "I knows every back road in Mississippi because we couldn't drive on the highways, the Highway Patrol was just as dangerous as the Klan." She talked of driving a gunshot victim to a hospital on the back roads. Of the dangers, she says, "Your freedom is important. We dying anyway, so you better die for something . . . it was worth it! It was nothing in vain."

The bus Unita and others rode on to the Democratic Convention in Atlantic City when they challenged the seating of the Mississippi delegation was paid for by Harry Belafonte and Sidney Poitier. She told me and the young people at the former Alex Haley Farm how one woman held a knife to the bus driver's neck to make him drive through the Klan roadblocks. She was also told about sitting in a church with Mrs. Fannie Lou Hamer deciding whether to take the compromise of two seats offered by the Democratic Credentials Committee in Atlantic City and how they decided to reject it.

Bob Moses told us, "That's up to y'all. Y'all are the people from Mississippi. You have to make that decision."

"We didn't leave there talking about no two seats," Mrs. Hamer said. "Girl, I wonder where we going to sit. All the rest of us, they going to give us two seats. All of us can't sit in them seats."

I said, That's the truth. I said We said half. "I say we say half," she said. "Well, you with me?" I said, We left there telling the folks what we was going to do. She looked at me and said, "We will not take the compromise." I say, That's it, go tell them.

And she went out and they was waiting on Fannie Lou. Miss Hamer went out and laid her head back and went to singing. She always sung them songs before she's going to hit you with a powerful message. And when she got through singing, the press had all them little things around sticking in her face. She just said, "We will NOT take the compromise." I thought some of our dear leaders would faint or fall out.

Without our ranks they told us we was ignorant. That we didn't know what we were doing. Them old ignorant folks from Mississippi, pick king cotton, but we changed the concept of how this nation do business in politics.

So, Miss Hamer was my mentor, my friend, my buddy. And she helped me spiritually too because she tried to teach me about hate. And so she told me I could not go around hating. Because that was not going to solve the problem. We have to love them.

⊰ 10 ⊱
MARTIN LUTHER KING, JR.,
AND R.F.K.

A Season of Hope for the Hungry

T HE COMBINED EXHILARATION and horror of Freedom Summer which opened to full view Mississippi's violent and oppressive society, obscured the snail's pace of change in the economic and political life in the state only for a short while. Eventually the lack of concrete progress was resented by impatient young Black people eager to loosen the noose of bondage. This and the cumulative stress and fatigue from chronic harassment and battle after battle, the disillusionment with the Democratic Party's politically pragmatic disregard for truth and justice in Atlantic City at the end of the summer of 1964, and the continuing White violence opened the door for the charismatic Stokely Carmichael and his Black Power allies to gain greater public voice and to push aside SNCC's courageous leader John Lewis in a de facto coup d'état. Some in SNCC began to replace Dr. King's nonviolent philosophy and "Freedom Now" cry with the Black Power fist and Malcolm X's cry, "By any means necessary." Differing expectations about goals and strategies to accelerate the pace of change, simmering for several years, burst into the open in 1966 after Ole Miss pioneer James Meredith was shot while attempting to walk from Memphis to Jackson.

Dr. King, Stokely Carmichael, and many other civil rights leaders and citizens converged on Mississippi to finish Meredith's march. I walked with them and listened in debriefings every evening after the march ended as Stokely and other SNCC members vented their frustrations at and to a saddened Dr. King who would shake his head at the embittered young turk and ask repeatedly, "Is it really that bad, Stokely?" Dr. King's stricken face in Greenwood, a SNCC stronghold, and on the platform in Jackson at the rally after the Meredith march was completed as SNCC leaders chanted "Black Power" is forever engraved in my mind's eye.

But Dr. King kept leading and preaching nonviolence and inspiring others to follow his way. I had joined him and thousands of fellow citizens walking from Selma and arriving in Montgomery on March 21, 1965 and was thrilled as Dr. King, "like Jonah in the belly of the whale," as James Washington wrote in his book *Testament of Hope*, "spoke triumphantly before the State Capitol building in Montgomery, often called the Cradle of Confederacy." As usual Dr. King captured our spirits by sharing the now immortalized words of a seventy-year-old Black woman, Sister Pollard, who when asked while walking during the Montgomery bus boycott if she wanted a ride answered, "No." When the person persisted, "Well, aren't you tired?" she responded, "My feets is tired, but my soul is rested."

The savage beatings and arrests of John Lewis, Hosea Williams, and others on Selma's Edmund Pettus Bridge days earlier provoked and galvanized over 25,000 marchers to answer Dr. King's call to complete the march in Montgomery and to ensure the voting rights of Black citizens. The sacrifices of James Reeb and Mrs. Viola Liuzzo, felled by racists' bullets, were rewarded in the witness of those undeterred by White violence. In Montgomery Dr. King cried, "My people, my people, listen! The battle is in our hands. The battle is in our hands in Mississippi and Alabama, and all over the United States." Warning of more suffering and jail cells ahead, he urged us to "go away more than ever before committed to the struggle and to nonviolence."

Later in 1965 Dr. King answered my call for help as Black Mississippi leaders and Head Start supporters struggled to convince Sargent Shriver and the Office of Economic Opportunity (OEO) he headed to renew funding for the Child Development Group of Mississippi (CDGM). CDGM had come into being when the state turned down

My father,
Arthur Jerome Wright,
as a young man.

My mother,
Maggie Leola Bowen Wright,
as a young woman.

Me, Marian Wright, as a junior bridesmaid at my sister Olive Wright's wedding to Heber Covington, Jr., at Shiloh Baptist Church in June 1950.

Some of the great women elders in my church and community during my childhood. Mrs. Theresa Kelly—Miz Tee—is in the middle of the back row with a black dress and white corsage.

Standing room only at one of my mother's many child-centered programs at Shiloh Baptist Church where my father served as pastor for twenty-five years.

Enjoying refreshments with friends after one of Mama's child pageants in "the hut"— the education building Daddy built for church activities.

Daddy and Mama sitting with Reverend Riddick—a very dignified man who needed a home after he lost his family and memory. Daddy and Mama began the first Black home for the aged in my hometown of Bennettsville, South Carolina. My mother continued and expanded it after my father died and my brother Julian continued it as the Arthur Jerome and Maggie Leola Wright Home for the Aged until he died. It continues today, operated by his daughters Stephanie and Crystal Wright.

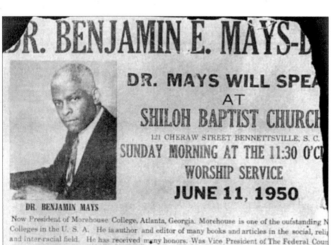

R. BENJAMIN E. MAYS-L

DR. MAYS WILL SPEA
AT
SHILOH BAPTIST CHURCH
121 CHERAW STREET BENNETTSVILLE, S. C.
SUNDAY MORNING AT THE 11:30 O'CL
WORSHIP SERVICE
JUNE 11, 1950

DR. BENJAMIN MAYS
Now President of Morehouse College, Atlanta, Georgia. Morehouse is one of the outstanding N
Colleges in the U. S. A. He is author and editor of many books and articles in the social, reli
and interracial field. He has received many honors. Was Vice President of The Federal Coun
Churches of Christ in America.

You can't afford to miss this opportunity of hearing one of the g
est minds and one of the most distinguished speakers of our ti

Promotion for an appearance by Dr. Benjamin Elijah Mays, president of Morehouse College, at Shiloh Baptist Church at Daddy's invitation. Dr. Mays stayed at our home and inspired my brother Harry to enroll at Morehouse College a few years later.

Me (second from left) and the members of my Lisle fellowship group with Soviet Premier Nikita Khrushchev at a village in the Caucasus during the summer of 1959. Fellow Spelman student Virginia Powell is to my left. It was the second U.S.—Soviet student exchange. I had witnessed Vice President Richard Nixon's and Premier Khrushchev's debate at the American Exhibition in Moscow a few weeks earlier.

Spelman College archives.

American photographer Edward Steichen and poet and writer Carl Sandburg before the entrance of the American Exhibition in Moscow in 1959. Daddy had bought Sandburg's multivolume biography of Abraham Lincoln for our home library and I was thrilled to meet the author of it.

(Left): Howard Zinn, my Spelman College history professor and mentor, at a book party for his book *LaGuardia in Congress. Spelman College archives.*

(Right): Charles E. Merrill, Jr., my lifelong mentor and chair of the Morehouse College board of trustees. His Merrill Fellowships enabled me and a number of Morehouse and Spelman College students and faculty members to travel and study abroad.
Spelman College archives.

(Opposite, top left): These notepad scribblings by Dr. Mays were tucked into my lost college diary. He was analyzing and applauding the Appeal for Human Rights drafted by students that preceded our sit-in demonstrations in Atlanta.

(Opposite, top right): This photo of Dr. Benjamin E. Mays was in my college diary along with my poem of admiration in chapter four. *Morehouse College Bulletin.*

(Opposite, bottom): Dr. Mays and I received honorary degrees together at commencement of the State University of New York at Old Westbury, where our dear friend and Freedom Rider John Maguire was president. I was *so* proud to be on the same stage with my hero. *Photograph by George H. Meyer.*

I was one of seventy-seven Black college students arrested for sitting in at public restaurants in Atlanta in March 1960. I led the student group that sat in at Atlanta's city hall. I kept calm in jail by reading C. S. Lewis's *The Screwtape Letters.*

Neatly stenciled sign on Interstate 55 overpass near McComb, Mississippi, recruiting members for the White supremacist Ku Klux Klan which encouraged violence against Black citizens. *Photograph by Matt Herron/TAKE STOCK.*

(Left): Children engaged in civil rights demonstrations in Jackson, Mississippi were among the many frontline child soldiers who helped transform America.

Photograph by Matt Herron/TAKE STOCK.

(Below): Children being taken in cattle trailers after being arrested in Jackson, Mississippi for protesting racial segregation and discrimination.

Photograph by Matt Herron/TAKE STOCK.

At a community meeting in Holmes County, Mississippi during my service as a civil rights attorney for the NAACP Legal Defense Education Fund. *Photograph by Moneta Sleet,* Ebony *magazine.*

Listening to and visiting families in Canton, Mississippi. *Photograph by Moneta Sleet,* Ebony *magazine.*

Visiting hungry children and families with Senator Robert F. Kennedy in the Mississippi Delta on April 11, 1967. CBS correspondent Daniel Schorr is in the background. Kennedy, outraged at the hunger and poverty he saw firsthand, set in motion a chain of events that eventually led to greatly expanded federal child and family nutrition programs.

AP/WIDE WORLD PHOTOS.

Robert Kennedy's exposure to hungry poor children and families in the Mississippi Delta led him to tell me to tell Dr. King to bring the poor to Washington. The Mule Train heading for Washington, D.C. from Marks, Mississippi for the Poor People's Campaign was the result. Dr. King's April 4, 1968 assassination dampened the campaign.

Photograph by Roland L. Freeman.

Children of Bertha Johnson: (back row) Brian, Terence, and Nelson; (front row) Trudy, Charles, Jr., and Brenda Marie at the Mule Train preparation site.

Photograph by Roland L. Freeman.

Peter's and my wedding on July 14, 1968, in Virginia. Ours was the first interracial marriage in Virginia since *Loving vs. Commonwealth* was decided by the United States Supreme Court, throwing out that state's antimiscegenation statute. Reverend William Sloane Coffin, Jr., officiated along with former U.S. Supreme Court Justice Arthur Goldberg, who kindly served as temporary flower girl. Justice Goldberg was Bill Coffin's attorney in his anti-Vietnam protest case.

In January 1968 I accompanied Robert G. Clark past the statue of the late segregationist Senator Bilbo in the lobby of the Mississippi State Capitol building where Clark was sworn in as the first Black member of the Mississippi House of Representatives since Reconstruction. *Corbis/Bettman—UPI.*

(Left): Mrs. Fannie Lou Hamer holding my son Joshua at his dedication to God ceremony, which reflected both parents' religious traditions.

(Below): Me with Mrs. Mae Bertha Carter at CDF's center for spiritual renewal and leadership development in Clinton, Tennessee, March 19, 1999, about a month before Mrs. Carter passed away.

Photograph by Todd Rosenberg.

My namesake Marian Anderson with Dr. Mary McLeod Bethune at the launching of the liberty ship S.S. *Booker T. Washington*, 1942. I was inspired by Dr. Bethune as a child.

Photographs and Prints Division, Schomburg Center for Research in Black Culture, The New York Public Library, Astor, Lenox and Tilden Foundations.

Miz Amie with our family, (left to right) Peter, Jonah, Joshua, Ezra, and me at home in Washington.

Marching across Memorial Bridge with my sons Jonah and Ezra at the first Stand for Children Day at the Lincoln Memorial on June 1, 1996. More than 250,000 people stood together to build the movement to Leave No Child Behind.® My son Jonah heads Stand for Children, a separately incorporated affiliate of the Children's Defense Fund. *Photograph by Rick Reinhard.*

Head Start money, uninterested in helping poor Black or White children. Arthur Thomas, head of the Delta Ministry of the National Council of Churches, Dr. Tom Levin, a psychiatrist from New York City interested in early childhood development, Dr. Daniel Biettel, the kind White president of all-Black Tougaloo College, and a group of local Black citizens from across the state worked together to help form the Child Development Group of Mississippi. It served about 13,000 children and created about 3,000 jobs free of the plantation system. I served as CDGM's counsel.

Helping poor children in Mississippi proved to be politically charged and complicated. Powerful Mississippi Senators Stennis and Eastland made their displeasure clear to Sargent Shriver and the Johnson White House and demanded they cut off CDGM funding. The senators alleged weak management and misuse of funds, the usual first course of attack when politicians want to inflict damage (the latter charge was not verified and the former was greatly overstated). CDGM's experience taught me a lesson I try never to forget: Be a good steward of every dime so that you're less vulnerable to political attack. Besides, the poor need to get their checks on time and good management is important to providing sound programs for children and families. As OEO began capitulating to political pressures from these powerful segregationist senators who threatened to hold up the appropriation for all OEO programs, we sought and found a counter political force in Walter Reuther and the United Auto Workers who supported the Citizens Crusade Against Poverty (CCAP) headed by Dick Boone. They became our Washington ally but still months dragged on without renewed funding.

CDGM parents and communities struggled to keep their centers open without federal funds as CDGM's board, staff, and I fought tirelessly to defend this lifeline of hope for thousands of Mississippi children. Shriver was furious when Dr. King walked into the room in Atlanta where he, I, and others were negotiating CDGM's fate and upbraided me and CDGM leaders for injecting "outsiders" into the process. But Dr. King's presence and announced support sent a message that we were prepared to fight with all our might and to mobilize as much support as we could to keep our community-based Head Start program alive. We won that 1965 refunding battle but faced a constant war of attrition during every refunding cycle. This included OEO encouraging the establishment of a rival more "controllable" group called MAP: Mississippi Action for Progress. This continuing attack on Mississippi Head Start programs was one impetus for my moving to Washington in 1968. I wanted to establish an ongoing voice and early alert system to protect the poor and vulnerable against the ruthless voices of powerful politicians seeking to maintain prevailing inequalities for the rich at the expense of the poor and for Whites at the expense of Blacks with government's help.

As Dr. King's struggle headed north, it ran into stiff resistance in Chicago and Cicero. And as the country became preoccupied with the Vietnam War, he spoke out against it in an eloquent speech on April 4, 1967 at Riverside Church in New York City. He eventually became discouraged both by stiff northern resistance to his civil rights campaigns and by stinging criticism from many Black and White leaders who thought Vietnam was none of his business and that he should express views only about "Black" issues. He rightly perceived the war's devastating effects on the hopes and needs of the poor at home. He correctly decried "taking the Black young men who had been crippled by our society and sending them 8,000 miles away to guarantee liberties in Southeast Asia which they had not found in Southwest Georgia and East Harlem."

●

Robert Kennedy came to Mississippi in that same April of 1967 with the Senate Subcommittee on Employment, Manpower, and Poverty chaired by Senator Joseph Clark of Pennsylvania and accompanied by Republican Senators Jacob Javits of New York and George Murphy of California. I had testified in Washington earlier about how the anti-poverty program in Mississippi was working before Chairman Joe Clark's committee at Senator Javits' request. Although I had intended to focus my Mississippi testimony on how well CDGM's Head Start program was helping poor children in the state's poorest counties, I had become increasingly concerned about the growing hunger in the Mississippi Delta.

The convergence of efforts to register Black citizens to vote, Black parents' challenges to segregated schools, the development of chemical weed killers and farm mechanization, and recent passage of a minimum wage law covering agriculture workers on large farms had resulted in many Black sharecroppers being pushed off their near feudal plantations which no longer needed their cheap labor. Indeed I believed and told the senators and anyone who would listen that Mississippi's power structure wanted Blacks not only to leave their plantations but to leave the state and go north. It didn't want the trouble of civil rights agitation. Many displaced sharecroppers were illiterate and had no skills. Free federal food commodities like cheese, powdered milk, flour, and peanut butter were all that stood between them and starvation. Their meager wages from the back-breaking work of chopping and picking cotton that often rewarded them only with more debt at the plantation owner's store had disappeared. Some had *no* income. Senators Eastland and Stennis and Congressman Jamie Whitten, who chaired the House Agriculture Committee, had supported the federal food commodity program for years when it subsidized Mississippi's political and economic bondage system. But as White Mississippi farmers and employers evicted Blacks who tried to register to vote, the economic vise was tightened in some counties by converting the free food commodity program into a newly created food stamp program. Like the swell-sounding "freedom of choice" school desegregation plans, food stamps carried some positive appeal: You could choose your own food in the grocery store rather than taking whatever was given out from federal surplus commodities resulting from federal subsidies (welfare) to farmers. But since food stamps required a minimum purchase price of $2.00 for a family of four, people with no income in Mississippi had no choice besides hunger which had escalated in Mississippi's Delta.

The state's stingy welfare program did not help two-parent families. Single mothers with two children were provided $56.00 a month as late as 1970; in 1998, they were provided $120 a month, a 48 percent reduction if you account for inflation. The rampant hypocrisy of segregationist politicians who railed against "lazy Blacks" did not deter them from collecting hefty federal welfare checks called price supports not to grow food hungry people needed to live. Often federal and state "subsidies" and tax incentives were and are simply words for government welfare for non-needy corporations, farmers, and citizens. Federal corporate welfare today exceeds $300 billion a year allegedly to make the rich more productive and work harder while the federal welfare safety net for poor mothers and children was shred during the 1996 election year allegedly to make poor mothers work harder. But adequate funds have not been invested in jobs with decent wages, job training, health care, child care, and transportation required to help them escape poverty. My historian friend Howard Zinn says all of modern history "shows a consistent record of laissez-faire for the poor, but enormous government intervention for the rich."

I shared the desperate plight of these hungry people with the senators in Jackson, Mississippi and urged them to go with me to the Delta to see for themselves the hungry poor in our very rich nation, to visit their shacks, open their empty cupboards, and look into the deadened eyes of children with bloated bellies. "They are starving and someone has to help them," I testified.

Robert Kennedy responded. In a precursor of the Children's Defense Fund's Child Watch visitation program which attempts to personalize child suffering by taking political, media, and community leaders to see the need and solutions to those needs firsthand, Robert F. Kennedy, Peter Edelman, his legislative assistant who was later to become my husband, and the national media who followed Kennedy, including Daniel Schorr, the distinguished CBS correspondent, traveled with me to the Mississippi Delta to visit poor families and children. Amzie Moore, always ready to help, immediately identified families for us to visit. We flew first to visit a small job-training program at the closed Greenville Air Base which I and others had been urging the federal government without success to let us use to house the evicted and homeless poor. We then drove to Cleveland, Mississippi where Amzie was waiting.

I was not prepared to like Robert Kennedy. I'd formed an image of him as a tough, arrogant, politically driven man from the Joseph McCarthy era. This view was reinforced later by the appointment while he was attorney general of a number of segregationist judges to southern federal courts, by his discouraging planned freedom rides and other civil rights demonstrations, and by his approval of wiretapping of Dr. King. I also had envisaged Peter Edelman, Kennedy's legislative assistant, as a cigar-chomping, arrogant young know-it-all as I then assumed most Kennedy staffers to be. These feelings dissolved as I saw Kennedy profoundly moved by Mississippi's hungry children. I liked Peter too!

Robert Kennedy went into houses asking respectfully of each dweller what they had had for breakfast, lunch, or dinner the night before. He opened their empty ice boxes and cupboards after asking permission. He hovered, visibly moved, on a dirt floor in a dirty shack out of television-camera range over a listless baby with bloated belly from whom he tried in vain to get a response. He lightly touched the cheeks, shoulders, and hands of the children clad in dirty ragged clothes and tried to offer words of encouragement to their hopeless mothers. From this trip and throughout the fifteen months I knew him until his assassination, I came to associate Robert Kennedy with nonverbal communications that conveyed far more than words: a light touch on the face, a pat on the shoulder, an affectionate gentle hit on the arm or back. He looked straight at you and he *saw* you. His capacity for genuine outrage and compassion was palpable. Later that day after our loud motorcade ran over a dog in Cleveland, Mississippi, he got out of the car to comfort a small boy to whom the dog belonged and angrily ordered the police escort to cut out the siren and to slow down.

Robert Kennedy was a teaser who was insatiably curious about everything including my personal life. As we drove from Greenville to Cleveland he asked about my dating life (I told him it was none of his business), about what I was reading (it happened to be Bill Styron's *The Confessions of Nat Turner*), what led me to come to Mississippi, and how I felt about numerous other topics.

He kept his word to help Mississippi's hungry children. Upon returning to Washington he went the next day with his legislative assistant Peter Edelman to see Secretary of Agriculture Orville Freeman to tell him what he'd seen and to "get the food down there." Anticipating and hearing Freeman's and other agriculture officials' skepticism that there were people in America with *no* income, he sent Peter Edelman back to Mississippi immediately with agriculture officials to see for themselves the penniless people with empty pantries he had visited. And so the Edelman family got its start. My husband and I often quip that we fell in love over hungry children.

Robert Kennedy's pushing, passion, and visibility set in motion a chain of events that culminated years later in the virtual elimination of hunger in America during the Nixon years. These included a series of expansions of child and family nutrition programs including the food stamp program that now reaches over twenty million Americans, a majority of whom are children. Agriculture Secretary Freeman, with confirmed documentation from his own staff that there were indeed people with *no* income, immediately changed regulations to permit this penniless group to get food stamps without charge. The Field Foundation of New York City, headed by a compassionate southerner, Leslie Dunbar, who gave CDF's parent organization its first grant, assembled a team of distinguished doctors including Dr. Robert Coles and Dr. Raymond Wheeler from Charlotte, North Carolina, who visited and examined hundreds of poor southern children and found not only hungry children but children suffering from diseases thought to exist only in underdeveloped countries: marasmus, rickets, kwashiorkor, pernicious anemia. Their subsequent testimony about their findings before Senator Clark's subcommittee in Washington prompted even Mississippi Senator Stennis to propose a token antihunger emergency measure of $10 million. More Senate subcommittee field hearings, including one in South Carolina in which Senator Ernest "Fritz" Hollings participated, and with the help of Dr. Donald Gatch of Beaufort, South Carolina, produced more evidence of child malnutrition and garnered a significant southern senator's support for expanding nutrition programs. CBS's "60 Minutes," at Robert Kennedy's urging, sent brilliant young documentary-maker Martin Carr to film hunger in America. Carr captured on camera a baby dying while being born to a malnourished mother. The powerful documentary which aired after Robert Kennedy's death helped build momentum to address hunger as did Senator George McGovern's Select Senate Committee hearings around the nation to investigate hunger in America.

Robert Kennedy, in addressing the hunger emergency, always understood that the real culprit was poverty and lack of good jobs. Decent wages, training, and education were necessary to provide hope for restless youths and unskilled older men and women left behind by a changing economy. We need to act on this understanding today. How sad that hunger returned to America as a result of sustained efforts initiated in the Reagan years to dismantle or cut safety-net programs for the poor including food stamps and remains at a time when the economy is booming.

The Poor People's Campaign

On one of my trips to Washington which included a visit with my by now very special friend Peter Edelman, Peter and I visited Hickory Hill to chat with Robert Kennedy. Sitting around the pool, I updated him on what was happening in Mississippi and shared my frustrations with the continuing unjust system of government and White resistance to change. I told him I was stopping by Atlanta to visit with Dr. King before returning home to Jackson, Mississippi.

Robert Kennedy told me to tell Dr. King to bring the poor to Washington to make their plight visible to the American people and to put pressure on President Lyndon Johnson to respond to their needs. A few hours later I sat talking with Dr. King in his unprepossessing SCLC office on Auburn Avenue in Atlanta. He was depressed and uncertain about where to go next. When I told him what Robert Kennedy had said, Dr. King's eyes lit up and he called me an angel sent by God. Thus the idea of the Poor People's Campaign for which I was honored to serve as messenger was born. Dr. King immediately began the hard work of convincing the SCLC staff that a Poor People's Campaign was a good idea and of putting together the massive recruitment efforts required to bring the poor to Washington. I brought over some poor people from Mississippi to meet with Dr. King and his SCLC staff which included Andy Young, Hosea Williams, and James Bevel, to help convince them of the merits of such a bold and demanding move to garner the attention of America to address poverty. Dr. King listened as his colleagues argued back and forth and then decided to proceed. Among the places he visited to urge people to go with him to Washington was muddy, unpaved Marks, Mississippi in Quitman County, where the pavement began where White folks lived and ended where Black folks lived.

On March 31, 1968 Dr. King gave a sermon, "Remaining Awake through a Great Revolution," at Washington's National Cathedral in which he told us: "We must all learn to live together as brothers or we will all perish together as fools." He cited technology, weaponry, and human rights as the three revolutionary changes requiring us to develop a world perspective and said: "We are tied together in the single garment of destiny, caught in an inescapable network of mutuality." "Somewhere," Dr. King preached, "we must come to see that human progress never rolls in on the wheels of inevitability. It comes through the tireless efforts and the persistent work of dedicated individuals who are willing to be co-workers with God" and that "the time is always ripe to do right." He reminded us of the story of "the rich man Dives and the beggar Lazarus. There is nothing in that parable that said Dives went to hell because he was rich . . . Dives went to hell because he passed by Lazarus every day and he never really saw him. He went to hell because he allowed his brother to become invisible . . . Dives went to hell because he sought to be a conscientious objector in the war against poverty." Just as Dives didn't realize that his wealth was his opportunity, he said America—the richest nation in the world—could make the same mistake. He said that the Poor People's Campaign "is America's opportunity to help bridge the gulf between the haves and the have nots. The question is whether America will do it. There is nothing new about poverty. What is new is that we now have the techniques and the resources to get rid of poverty. The real question is whether we have the will." That is still the real and urgent question in an $8.6 trillion American economy that has quadrupled in wealth since Dr. King spoke but lets fourteen million children live in poverty.

Four days after his impassioned plea for America to help the poor he was dead—assassinated in Memphis trying to help striking sanitation workers. I will never forget the surreal days that followed, especially the funeral cortege behind the simple pine pauper's box carrying his body; Dr. Mays' moving eulogy to our slain young prophet;

and the haunting voices of Morehouse College's choir saluting their departed brother with "Dear Old Morehouse," the same school song they had serenaded him with as his plane had departed three years earlier for Oslo to accept the Nobel Peace Prize.

Robert Kennedy slipped quietly into Ebenezer Church to view Dr. King's body the night before the funeral and walked in the procession from Ebenezer to the campuses of Atlanta University and Morehouse after the funeral the next day. He had recently announced his decision to run for president and had been campaigning in Indiana when news came of Dr. King's assassination. He movingly shared the terrible news with the waiting crowd of mostly Black citizens, urging them not to hate and reminding them that a White man had killed his brother too.

Our dark, deep despair at Dr. King's death was leavened only by the fact that we still had Robert Kennedy who if elected president might not only end the war in Vietnam but finish the needed war against poverty. And we had the tasks of carrying out the Poor People's Campaign without Dr. King. But two months and two days later, Robert Kennedy died from an assassin's bullet on my birthday, June 6, 1968. I never wore the lovely bracelet my fiancé Peter Edelman had bought at the Ambassador Hotel in Los Angeles as a birthday present.

As I walked into St. Patrick's Cathedral in New York City where Robert Kennedy's body lay in state, a weeping Charles Evers, slain Medgar's brother, clung to me asking over and over, "What are we going to do now?" Riding on the train from New York City to Washington, D.C. bearing Robert Kennedy's body, I was deeply moved by the stricken faces of young and old, Black and White who lined the funeral train route who mirrored my stricken heart. The single most poignant moment for me was when the hearse carrying Robert Kennedy's body to rest beside his brother John Kennedy at Arlington National Cemetery moved towards Memorial Bridge. It paused for a moment to allow the poor people remaining in muddy Resurrection City from the Poor People's Campaign who were standing at attention near the Lincoln Memorial to bid farewell. It was Robert Kennedy's last campaign.

◆

On April 5, 1968, in Cleveland, Ohio, following Dr. King's assassination, Robert F. Kennedy spoke about "the mindless menace of violence in America which again stains our land and every one of our lives. It is not," he said, "the concern of any one race. The victims of the violence are black and white, rich and poor, young and old, famous and unknown. They are most important of all, human beings who other human beings loved and needed. No one—no matter where he lives or what he does—can be certain who will suffer from some senseless action of bloodshed. And yet it goes on and on and on in this country of ours."

Since Robert Kennedy spoke those words, he and over 936,000 American men, women, and children have been killed by guns. Another 550,000 Americans have died violent deaths by other means in America's undeclared twentieth-century civil war. This twenty-nine-year 1.4 million death toll of American against American and of Americans who, unable to face life or find love, hope, purpose, or safe haven in family, community, faith, or democratic civic life, took their own lives, is more than three times the number of reported American battle deaths in all of the wars in the twentieth century. Between 1968 and 1996, fewer than 32,000 American soldiers died in military conflicts in other countries. We Americans were forty-four times more likely to kill each other and ourselves than to be killed by an external enemy.

Gun violence has never been and is not now just or primarily an inner-city Black problem as Littleton, Colorado, Pearl, Mississippi, Jonesboro, Arkansas, Paducah, Kentucky, Springfield, Oregon, Edinboro, Pennsylvania, and Conyers and Atlanta, Georgia have reminded us. Approximately half of the 405,176 gun homicide victims between 1968 and 1996 were White (196,041) and half were Black (201,808), and 92 percent of the 465,661 (428,408) gun suicide victims were White. Most of these gun deaths were not caused by strangers but by neighbors or acquaintances or were self-inflicted. Guns have lethalized our moments of despair and anger and turned temporary bouts of emotional instability into tragic permanent losses.

Most shamefully, between 1979 and 1996, over 75,000 American *children* have been killed and 375,000 *children* have been wounded by guns. Twenty thousand more American children died and 225,000 more children were wounded by firearms on the killing fields of America than American soldiers died and were wounded on the killing fields of Vietnam.

What has happened to us that the morally unthinkable killing of innocent children has become routine not only in Bosnia and Brazil, Rwanda and Kosovo but in New York City, Detroit, and Chicago? Nearly 13 children in our country are killed by guns daily—a classroomful of children every two days. American children under fifteen are twelve times more likely to die from gunfire than their peers in twenty-five other industrialized countries *combined*, the Centers for Disease Control and Prevention reports. How many little ones is it going to take for America to stand up and stop the killing of children? What is it going to take for you to say enough and to act?

Even our youngest children cannot escape gun violence. Between 1979 and 1996, three times more children under five (1,875) were killed than American soldiers in action (505). In 1996, 55 law enforcement officers were killed in the line of duty while 4,600 children were gunned down. Homicide is now the third leading cause of death among children five to fourteen years old, the second leading cause of death among children and young adults ten to twenty-four, and the leading cause of death among Black teen males and females. More young Black males are killed by guns each year than died from all the lynchings throughout American history. Where is our antiviolence campaign, Black community and America?

Escalating violence against and by children and youth is no coincidence. It is the cumulative, convergent, and heightened manifestation of a range of serious and too-long neglected and denied problems. Epidemic poverty; increasing economic inequality; racial, religious, and gender intolerance and hate crimes; rampant drug and alcohol abuse; violence in our homes and glorification of violence in our popular culture, toys, and video games; large numbers of teen and adult out-of-wedlock births and divorces; and overly busy and stressed-out parents have all contributed to the disintegration of the family, community, and spiritual values and supports all children need. Add to these crises easier and easier access to deadlier and deadlier firearms; hordes of lonely and neglected children and youths left to fend for themselves by absentee parents in all race and income groups; gangs and cliques of alienated inner-city and suburban youths relegated to the margins of family, school, and depersonalized community institutions without enough sound home training, education, purpose, jobs, or hope; and political leadership in all parties and at all levels that pays more attention to foreign than domestic enemies, to the rich than to the poor, to their own political survival than to our children's survival, and you face the social and spiritual disintegration of American society that I believe we are witnessing today.

What are the real family values in the richest nation on earth that lets one in five of its children live in poverty and allows children to be the poorest group of Americans? What must God think about citizens and leaders with a booming nearly $9 trillion economy that lets children suffer hunger, homelessness, sickness, illiteracy, injury, and death that we have the means but not the will to prevent?

What does national security mean to millions of children who witness violence at home and in the streets every year and to the million children who themselves are abused and neglected?

I wonder how many of the fifteen-year-old murderers today were born without adequate prenatal care and nutrition because our nation claimed we could not afford to give them a Healthy Start? How many sixteen-year-old teen mothers having babies today entered school not ready to learn because we would not invest early in a Head Start for them? How many eighteen-year-old murderers witnessed and suffered abuse and neglect at home from parents who were never nurtured themselves, taught to parent, trained to work, or able to earn enough to escape poverty when they did work? Seventy percent of poor children live in a household where someone works. How many nineteen-year-old youths abusing and pushing drugs today are children who saw the adults in their lives abusing or pushing drugs and who lacked positive community alternatives to dysfunctional families and dangerous streets? How much competition are our religious congregations and community institutions providing youths to combat the drug dealers and gun sellers and gangs and violent video, movie, and television wares available to our children twenty-four hours a day, seven days a week that desensitize our children to the consequences of violence? Where are the parental and community mentors to lure restless youths into fun, learning, and service and away from the crass exploitation of children as consumers?

All adults are responsible for protecting children and contributing public safety. It is time to pierce the NRA myths about Second Amendment protection of private gun ownership and to organize to protect children instead of guns. There is *no* excuse for the unbridled trafficking in nonsporting handguns, assault weapons, and ammunition. It is insane that a gun is produced or imported in America about every eight seconds and that more than 200 million guns are legally in the hands of Americans—many concealed. It makes no sense that our nation regulates the safety of countless products including children's toy guns, teddy bears, blankets, and pajamas and does not regulate the safety of a product that killed over thirty thousand American children and adults in 1996 and injured many more. Why are guns the only unregulated consumer product in America? Why do we require a license to drive a car and registration to own a car but not to own a gun?

Our failure to control the proliferation of arms and to confront the plague of violence which permeates our culture has weakened the moral thresholds which hold societies together. The traditional rules and boundaries of war have disappeared in Rwanda, Kosovo, and in the United States as innocent civilians, humanitarian workers, and women and children are slaughtered indiscriminately by guns and bombs. Even a mother's womb no longer shields babies against violent assault. A Detroit pediatrician wrote in 1993: "We have seen 22 pregnant adolescents with gun shot wounds in two small inner-city hospitals in Detroit."

Dr. King and Robert Kennedy lived and died trying to address these plagues of physical and spiritual poverty. It is time for us to hear and act.

⊰ 11 ⊱

MOVEMENT TIME

⬥

ANDREW YOUNG called Dr. King "a very reluctant and reactive prophet." He did not initiate the Montgomery bus boycott, the March on Washington, the student sit-ins, the march from Selma to Montgomery, or the Poor People's Campaign. But he melded them all together with other campaigns into a powerful movement which he embodied and symbolized.

Dorothy Cotton, the charismatic education director for Dr. King's Southern Christian Leadership Conference, says, "Movement is people in motion for a particular purpose." A movement is a dynamic ragged eruption that bubbles up over time in the consciousness of many people from many different places who feel a common grievance or need or shared suffering. It is like lava in a volcano that finally erupts. World War I and World War II's Black soldiers like my Daddy came home from defending our democracy in Europe too restless and changed to accept the old ways at home. Charles Houston and Thurgood Marshall and a small brilliant band of Black lawyers began carefully and methodically to conceptualize and implement a legal strategy to end public education apartheid. Beginning with *Sweatt v. Painter*, they challenged grossly unequal and segregated higher education for Blacks in Texas. Their legal odyssey culminated in *Brown v. Board of Education* in 1954 outlawing racially segregated public schools.

Mrs. Rosa Parks' courage in refusing to get up and give her seat to a White man ignited the Montgomery bus boycott. Mrs. Parks was not by any means the first Black person to sit down in the front of a segregated bus in the South. My friend and legal scholar, the late Pauli Murray, author of *Proud Shoes*, and I often shared stories during Yale Law School days about our protests against segregated public transportation. Pauli's protest in Washington, D.C. preceded Mrs. Parks' by many years. When I was a freshman returning at night from my first interracial seminar at the Atlanta YMCA, I sat down in the front of the bus. I am sure Mrs. Parks' Montgomery example had affected me but my panic-stricken Black Spelman chaperone begged me not to cause trouble so I relented somewhat by standing in the aisle halfway between the White and Black sections. I remember gazing at the empty seats before and behind me and feeling enraged at the stupidity of the South's dehumanizing racial caste system.

Who knows what emboldened Mrs. Parks in 1955 not to move after riding segregated buses all her life? Was it her tired feet or her tired soul saying *enough*, or the seeds from the Highlander Folk School citizenship training she had attended some weeks before, or all of these? Perhaps sharing time and grievances with others from across the South and feeling part of a community of fellow strugglers unleashed long repressed emotions and courage.

Mrs. Parks was just the right person at the right time to light the spark that lit the movement that Montgomery NAACP head E. B. Nixon had been vigilantly working, watching, and waiting for. He had a plan and an infrastructure ready to go when the right case and opportunity arose. Who knows whether and when a movement in Montgomery would have swelled up without an E. B. Nixon and his organizational capacity to translate an incident into a community-wide mobilization. He understood and shared the simmering discontent of Montgomery's Black community about their oppressive segregated environment. And E. B. Nixon recognized the crucial role that Black churches and ministers could play in mobilizing the Black community to challenge segregation. Without a strong moral base, movements cannot soar or be sustained over time.

It was E. B. Nixon who anointed the young Martin Luther King, Jr., who had just arrived in Montgomery, rather than Reverend Ralph Abernathy or another more established Montgomery pastor to lead the movement and rally the people. "God has," Andy Young says, "ways of acting anonymously" to set the stage for the workings of His justice. God chooses the actors, the times, the places, sets the stage, lifts the curtain, and begins the drama. Our task is to be ready to play our parts and to do the work God assigns us without anxiety according to the strengths and gifts we are given.

There might not have been a Civil Rights Movement so soon or so sweeping without a King or a Parks or a Nixon, or a Houston or a Marshall whose legal groundwork came to fruition in *Brown*. The movement might have died out without Black college students like Ezell Blair in Greensboro, Diane Nash in Nashville, and hundreds of others who said it's time to sit down and eat without discrimination. I was among them, waiting for an outlet, inspired by what had happened in Montgomery. I cannot ever remember a time when I did not detest segregation and I knew one day that I would find a way to fight it. The sit-ins became that outlet.

The movement might have petered out if freedom riders, Black and White, had given up or if brave people like Diane Nash, Jim Bevel, James Farmer, Jim Peck, and others hadn't insisted on continuing them despite President Kennedy's and Robert Kennedy's reluctance. The movement might have ground to a halt and the Civil Rights Act of 1964 might never have been enacted if A. Philip Randolph had not threatened to march on President Franklin Delano Roosevelt's Washington in 1941 and finally did it twenty-two years later in President Kennedy's and Dr. King's time with Bayard Rustin's brilliant coordination. It might have died before the Voting Rights Act was enacted if Diane Nash, Jim Bevel, John Lewis, Hosea Williams, and others had not courageously responded to the cruel bombing of Birmingham's 16th Street Baptist Church by planning to march across the Edmund Pettus Bridge from Selma to Montgomery and if Dr. King and thousands of others had not finished their quest after the first marchers were brutally attacked. It might have waned if Bob Moses and his SNCC co-workers had not gone to Mississippi and tried to register poor Black citizens to vote at risk of life and limb. It also might have faltered if SNCC, with Al Lowenstein's help, had not recruited White students to join Black citizens in the Mississippi freedom struggle; SNCC gained national visibility by enlisting the middle-class White youths America cared more about. The chronic racial violence against Blacks in Mississippi might never have received a national response if two White mothers' sons hadn't joined one Black mother's son in being ambushed and murdered by lynchers wearing law enforcement badges in Philadelphia, Mississippi. This racist reality is reflected again in response to White youth shootings in suburban schools, although Black children have been dying from guns for years largely unnoticed.

The Montgomery movement might have stalled and ended through attrition if organized national legal groups like the NAACP Legal Defense Fund—with a national vision and strategy—and its local cooperating attorneys like Fred Gray had not won the legal case which ended racial segregation on Montgomery buses and came as a Godsend to the young King. How long before tired feet would have become tired wills if some success could not have been shown?

And the movement might never have realized its enormous potential to transform southern politics if Ella Baker and Septima Clark had not picked up where Mrs. Rosa Parks left off. Mrs. Baker understood that individual marches and demonstrations without organizational infrastructure and a larger strategy or vision could not engage a critical mass of people or institutionalize change. Mrs. Septima Clark understood that the ability to read was essential if exercising the right to vote was to become real. And there might have been no movement without the preaching and mass meetings and music like Mrs. Fannie Lou Hamer's singing "This Little Light of Mine, I'm Going to Let It Shine" that held us together as a community of ragged and often scared activists, giving us courage and spiritual nourishment. Zylphia Horton and Guy Carawan's adaptation of "We Shall Overcome" from a Negro spiritual became the theme song of the Civil Rights Movement and helped drown out our fears of the dogs and hoses and mean White mobs and police and Klan. The music allowed us to tell God all about our troubles and hopes, to plead with God to guide our feet, hold our hands, bolster our lagging determination, and quell our doubts.

If many faith groups and affluent supporters like Harry Belafonte and Sidney Poitier had not raised money for bail, if ordinary people hadn't displayed extraordinary hospitality and courage in opening up their humble homes and sharing their beds and loaves and fishes with "outsiders" like me (I was the third person sharing a bed in a Mississippi shack on my first visit as a student), and if poor families hadn't shared what they had with strangers, the movement may not have survived and thrived.

Too many of our children in inner-city, suburban, and rural areas, in Ivy League, Black, and other institutions of higher education, do not know about the movement that crumbled America's racial Berlin Wall. Too few Whites and Blacks alike remember beyond a Martin Luther King holiday celebration or reading Dr. King's still unrealized great dream of an America that judges children by "the content of their character rather than by the color of their skin" and enables *all* children to achieve their God-given potential. Dr. King believed that America could provide a roof over every citizen's head, an education for their minds, a job to support their families, and freedom to pray and grow and sing and worship and feed their spirit. He led us towards that land promised in the Declaration of Independence but could not stay to go with us. But in Memphis in his last speech he promised us we would get there. It is time for us to cross over.

❧ 12 ❧
GREAT BLACK WOMEN
MENTORS AND MOVEMENT
BUILDERS

*Harriet Tubman, Sojourner Truth,
Mary McLeod Bethune,
Septima Clark, and Ella Baker*

I ALWAYS KNEW and heard about strong and accomplished Black women when I was growing up. I write here about Harriet Tubman and Sojourner Truth, Mary McLeod Bethune and Septima Clark and Ella Baker.

Ida B. Wells, who helped end lynchings that took over 3,400 Black lives in this century, and who would be appalled to know that more young Black males under twenty-five today die from guns every year, was held up to me as well. I learned about Nannie Helen Burroughs, Charlotte Hawkins Brown, and Elizabeth Evelyn Wright who started schools to educate Black children since White public schools excluded them completely or educated them unequally. They would be leading the fight today for our poor Black children, one of whom drops out of school every fifty seconds, and standing up to those both inside and outside our public school systems who do not expect or help our children to learn.

Anna Julia Cooper, who received her Ph.D. at the Sorbonne at a time when few Black or White women even went to college, later served as principal of the superb M Street School in Washington, D.C.

Today she would be telling Black children in the nation's capital about the vibrant Black renaissance period on the U Street corridor and in the Shaws/Le Droit Park/Howard University neighborhood where Duke Ellington lived and played, and Jean Toomer and Langston Hughes and Sterling Brown and Paul Lawrence wrote and read their works, and Black intellectuals from Howard and political leaders debated issues affecting Black and American life and created poems and novels that we need to read and learn from today.

I understood early that if Black women had not done what they always do—most of the organizing and scut work—while men got most of the credit and publicity, our families and communities would not have held together through slavery and segregation. Black mothers never lost sight of the holy seed in the stump after slavery's destruction tried to chop off the limbs of our humanity. Black mothers and grandmothers never stopped dreaming and working towards a world where in Langston Hughes' great poem, "Whatever race you be, will share the bounties of the earth and every man is free."

Brave Black girls like Linda Brown and Prathia Hall and Sophia Bracey challenged segregated schools in court and in school, and a little six-year-old girl like Ruby Bridges in New Orleans and Deborah Lewis and the Carter children in Mississippi endured mean White heckling day after day as they sat alone or in classrooms where others mistreated them in order to achieve the better education that *Brown v. Board of Education* promised.

Mrs. Parks sat down and refused to move from her bus seat, and the Civil Rights Movement was ignited. Montgomery's Black community wouldn't have stood up to end segregation in public transportation in America without her witness. Montgomery Black women walked to their jobs as maids or found means other than buses to get where they needed to go with the help of some White women like the feisty Virginia Durr whose husband Clifford Durr got Mrs. Parks out of jail. All of these women, sung and unsung, helped the boycott succeed and raised up a new young leader named Martin Luther King, Jr., to be our greatest twentieth-century national prophet.

HARRIET TUBMAN AND SOJOURNER TRUTH

As a child, I read books about Harriet Tubman and the underground railroad and knew there was a fearless former slave woman named Sojourner Truth. After becoming chair of Spelman's board of trustees, I convinced fellow trustees to name the two concourses in our new student center after these two unlettered but extraordinary Black women freedom fighters so that generations of Spelman women leaders would know their names, remember their legacies, and carry forth their struggles for justice.

Harriet Tubman and Sojourner Truth represent the thousands of anonymous women whose voices were muted by slavery, segregation, and confining gender roles throughout history. Harriet Tubman freed herself from slavery then went back South through forests and streams and across mountains countless times to lead fellow slaves to freedom. She was tough. She was determined. She was fearless. She was shrewd. Harriet Tubman trusted God completely to deliver her and her fellow slaves from their pursuing captors who had placed a bounty on her life. " 'Twa'nt me. 'Twas the Lord. I always told Him, I trust You. I don't know where to go or what to do, but I expect You to lead me. And He always did. . . . On my underground railroad, I never ran my train off the track and I never lost a passenger," she was quoted as saying. No train, bus company, or airline can match this slave woman's record and partnership with God.

What Frederick Douglass wrote to Harriet Tubman on August 28, 1868 eloquently summed up her life and that of so many Black women:

The difference between us is very marked. Most that I have done and suffered in the service of our cause has been in public, and I have received much encouragement at every step of the way. You, on the other hand, have labored in a private way. I have wrought in the day—you the night. I have had the applause of the crowd and the satisfaction that comes of being approved by the multitude, while the most that you have done has been witnessed by a few trembling, scared, and foot-sore bondmen and women, whom you have led out of the house of bondage, and whose heartfelt "God bless you" has been your only reward. The midnight sky and the silent stars have been the witness of your devotion to freedom.

Like Harriet Tubman, Sojourner Truth was a brilliant but illiterate slave woman, a great orator and powerful presence who also possessed great courage. She challenged the racial and gender caste system of slavery by suing for the return of a son sold away from her. She got thrown off but kept getting back on Washington, D.C. streetcars until they let her ride. She stood up with fiery eloquence to opponents and threatening crowds who tried to stop her from speaking. When a hostile White man told her that the hall where she was scheduled to speak would be burnt down if she spoke she replied, "Then I will speak to the ashes." When taunted while speaking in favor of women's rights by some White men who asked if she was really a woman, she bared her breasts and famously retorted, "Ain't I a woman?," detailing the back-breaking double burden of slavery's work and childbearing she had endured. When heckled by a White man in her audience who said he didn't care any more about her antislavery talk than for an old flea bite, she snapped back, "Then the Lord willing, I'll keep you scratching." And when decrying her exclusion from America's life and Constitution she asked, "God, what ails this Constitution? I feels for my rights and don't feel any there." She said God replied, "'Sojourner, there some little weasels in it.'"

Since Sojourner Truth's day, Black and White and Brown and other excluded and marginalized women have been trying to ferret out the weasels in the Constitution and our national life and to build a just America and world for themselves and their children. That effort must accelerate and reach a mighty roar.

MARY MCLEOD BETHUNE

Dr. Mary McLeod Bethune completely commanded the dinner table at Benedict College as she recounted stories about straightening out White folks as I sat listening as a young girl. When a White hat shop clerk attempted to prevent her from trying on a hat Dr. Bethune asked her, "Do you know who I am? I am Mary McLeod Bethune." In the South, Black customers were expected to look, buy, but not try on clothes or sit down for lunch while shopping. It was from Mrs. Bethune that I first heard the saying, "The blacker the berry the sweeter the juice." She exuded great pride in her God-painted very Black skin.

The power of her forceful personality in a room—even one mostly full of men who listened very attentively to her—never left me. She was confident about who she was, proud of what she had achieved, and never ashamed of where she came from. She built Bethune-Cookman College on top of a garbage dump with faith, will, and an initial investment of five dollars. It has educated thousands of Black youths since then and continues today. She founded the National Council of Negro Women, and her successor, my dear friend and role model Dorothy Height, carried it on with brilliance and dignity for forty-one years and still serves as its chair. Mrs. Bethune was friend to Eleanor Roosevelt through whom she would transmit messages to President Franklin Roosevelt that "the President needs to see me!"

One of my favorite Bethune stories was her reply to a White train conductor who called her "Auntie" and asked whether she could cook biscuits. She answered, "I am Dr. Mary McLeod Bethune. I am a college president, a founder of a national women's organization, and a friend of the President of the United States. And yes, I also can cook good biscuits."

I thought about this many decades later when I was sitting alone in an Aspen, Colorado restaurant, peacefully reading a book and drinking a cup of coffee when a White woman about my age disturbed me to announce she was looking for a maid and was I interested. I asked her how much she was paying and then told her what I would cost. I was not as gracious as Mrs. Bethune.

SEPTIMA CLARK

Without Septima Clark's foresight in teaching illiterate Black citizens to read so that they could vote on John's Island, South Carolina, Dr.

King's Southern Christian Leadership Conference would not have a training infrastructure to provide the skills for illiterate Black citizens to gain the right to vote, a process that transformed southern politics. Septima Clark took her citizenship school model to the Highlander Folk School begun by Myles Horton near Knoxville, Tennessee, where she became Highlander's education director. Mrs. Rosa Parks attended one of these Highlander training sessions shortly before she triggered the Montgomery bus boycott. Mrs. Parks later acknowledged Septima Clark's important role, noting that she had sat down once, but Septima Clark kept on working and building: "I am always very respectful and very much in awe of the presence of Septima Clark because her life story makes the effort that I have made very minute. I only hope that there is a possible chance that some of her great courage and dignity and wisdom has rubbed off on me. When I first met her in 1955 at Highlander, when I saw how well she could organize and hold things together in this very informal setting of interracial living, I had to admire this great woman. She just moved through the different workshops and groups as though it was just what she was made to do, in spite of the fact that she had to face so much opposition in her home state and lost her job and all of that. She seemed to be just a beautiful person, and it didn't seem to shake her."

Mrs. Septima Clark was one of eight children born in Charleston, South Carolina in 1898 of a former slave father. "I was forty-nine when the Civil Rights Movement really got going, both for me personally and for people all over the South," she said in *Ready from Within*. She had been teaching children in public schools since 1947. About the time Mrs. Parks sparked the Montgomery bus boycott, Septima Clark was facing the loss of her job. She had joined the NAACP and sought equalization of salaries for Black and White teachers in South Carolina. She said the biggest failure of her life was not persuading Black teachers who were afraid of losing their jobs to join the NAACP and her struggle for equal justice.

After Federal District Court Judge Waties Waring, following the law rather than White southern mores, ordered equal pay for Black and White teachers and also ruled that Black citizens must be permitted to vote in the next primary, he and his wife and Septima became friends and social pariahs in their community. When Septima asked the judge's wife to speak at her YWCA and Mrs. Waring accepted, both women received obscene calls. Neither backed down although the Warings eventually did leave Charleston after increasing harassment.

Myles Horton, Highlander's wonderful folk school head, said that Septima Clark did not let anyone or anything discourage her. She did not let the timidity of her Black friends in South Carolina who criticized her friendship with the Warings discourage her. She did not let the false label of Communist that White segregationists put on Highlander stop her. She did not let her arrest on a spurious charge intended to shut down Highlander's interracial activities discourage her. She did not let the sexism of some of the men on SCLC's staff discourage her: "The men on it [the executive staff] didn't listen to me too well. . . . They just thought that women were sex symbols and had no contribution to make." She says that Rev. Ralph Abernathy kept asking Dr. King why she was on staff.

Septima Clark knew education was the foundation of citizenship. She traveled tirelessly across the deep South teaching illiterate Black citizens to read in two or three months while also teaching them to stand up for their rights. She trained hundreds of other citizenship education teachers, providing not only the model but helping to build the community capacity needed to translate legal rights into political realities.

And she did not let two heart attacks or aging discourage her. She won her second term on the Charleston, South Carolina school board in 1976 as she celebrated her seventy-eighth birthday. She was the first Black woman ever to serve on that board.

The photographer Brian Lanker's cover of his marvelous book of photographs and essays on Black women, *I Dream a World*, captured this great woman's indomitable spirit a few weeks before her death. Septima Clark not only dreamed of but worked tirelessly for a world where every child is well educated and respected and loved as God intends. She told Brian, "I'd tell the children of the future that they have to stand up for their rights. They have an idea that they can. But I feel that they are shadows underneath a great shelter and that they need to come forth and stand up for some of the things that are right."

Mrs. Ella Baker

Andy Young told a group gathered at the former Alex Haley Farm that some of Dr. King's SCLC staff "could not stand Ella Baker." "When she heard I was planning to go to work for him, she called my mother and told her not to let me come. She thought we were all trifling and undisciplined and that included Martin and Ralph!" Andy continued, "We could deal with Septima because she reminded us of our grandmothers. We could deal with Dorothy [Dorothy Cotton, who co-directed with Andy Young Dr. King's citizenship education program] because she reminded us of our sisters. But we could not deal with Ella Baker because she reminded us of our mothers. She held us accountable and tolerated no nonsense. None of us had come to grips yet with our mothers."

Ella Baker was tough and disciplined and demanded the best of the young and older adults around her. I recently found a letter I had written to her apologizing for not getting a report I had promised in on time. She understood that movement building was about more than protests and meetings and speeches—it was hard, daily, persistent, behind-the-scenes work and infrastructure.

Mrs. Ella Baker was born in 1903 in Norfolk, Virginia. Like Septima Clark, she had a strict mother, a warm and caring father, and a large extended family of grandparents, uncles, and aunts who shared what they had with the poor. She was a fighter and as a child beat up White children who called her names. Since there was no schooling beyond elementary years where she lived, she went off to boarding school at Shaw University in Raleigh, North Carolina, where she graduated valedictorian of her high school and college classes. She moved to Harlem, got caught up in its excitement, and went everywhere to hear speeches, read in libraries, and to learn. After working as a domestic and as a waitress, she got a job with the *Negro National News* pub-

lished by George Schuyler who later recommended her for a job at the
NAACP. She rapidly rose through NAACP ranks. "Wherever she
went," her biographer and friend Joanne Grant wrote in *Ella Baker:
Freedom Bound*, "she created a whirlwind, leaving a scatter of papers,
notes, leaflets, church programs, and phone numbers in her wake. . . .
She never let up her struggle to increase the role of the rank and file."

Ella Baker pushed for structure and rules in the NAACP just as she
did later at SCLC and SNCC. I met her during my senior year at Spelman College when she was working in Atlanta for SCLC.

It was Ella Baker who sat down with Bayard Rustin and Stanley Lev-
inson to discuss how to create a continuing movement out of the
Montgomery bus boycott that led to SCLC's formation. It was Ella
Baker who tried to put SCLC in operating order so that Dr. King was
not just a leader who reacted to and jumped from one event to the
other, and who worked to give SCLC the capacity to plan and implement and not just react to change. It was Ella Baker who convinced Dr.
King to bring me and about two hundred other Black college students
from around the South who had been arrested for engaging in sit-in
protests to open up lunch counters to her alma mater Shaw University.
It was Ella Baker who encouraged students to form our own organization rather than simply becoming the youth arm of SCLC. It was Ella
Baker who warned against SCLC becoming "a cult of personality" for
Dr. King rather than an organized means of empowering others.

I remember her counsel as I think about sustaining and strengthen-
ing the Children's Defense Fund's crucial mission in the twenty-first
century. She taught me the crucial importance of training a successor
generation of young servant leaders which is now an integral and urgent part of CDF's mission and that of the Black Community Crusade
for Children (BCCC) which CDF coordinates.

Like Septima Clark, Ella Baker was fully aware of but unintimi-
dated by the men who resented her forcefulness, prodding, and
"mothering." She made no special effort to be ingratiating. She labored at SCLC as she had at the NAACP to raise money, conduct voter
registration drives, speak to citizen groups (sometimes ten times a
day), and travel to community after community to help people help

themselves. She eventually left SCLC after deciding that movement building was more important than the specific organization and personalities involved.

With Bob Moses and Jane Stembridge, I drove Ella Baker in my brother Julian's well-worn Volkswagen Beetle in August 1963 from New York City to Washington for the March on Washington. We stayed with my sister Olive and shared that period of hopefulness that Dr. King's dream, which was our own, could be realized in America in our lifetimes with the help of our hands and feet and voices.

At a gathering celebrating Ella Baker's seventy-fifth birthday, Bob Moses called her the "Fundi," the person in the community who masters a craft with the help of the community and teaches it to other people. She died in 1988 on her eighty-third birthday.

In 1991 at BCCC's invitation Black students convened at Howard University to organize a Black Student Leadership Network for Children (BSLN). Since then over 2,000 Black college-age youths have gone through training at BCCC's Ella Baker Child Policy Institute. These young leaders have operated summer Freedom Schools for over 12,000 poor children. They teach reading, conflict resolution, chess, provide two nutritious meals, and engage parents in churches, schools, and community centers in over forty-five sites across the country. The young leaders also serve as important role models for the children in their communities. Children do not need Michael Jordan as a role model, as extraordinary as he is. They need someone who grew up near them in their own communities who faced and overcame some of the same tough problems they now face and must overcome and who are giving back. Ella Baker would be proud of these young servant-leaders if she were alive today. We hope from their ranks many potential Ella Bakers, Septima Clarks, Andy Youngs, and Bob Moseses will emerge. The BSLN has evolved into the SLNC—the Student Leadership Network for Children—as we seek to engage more Latino, White, and Asian as well as Black students in the crusade to Leave No Child Behind.

◆

Black women must come together again and reach out to all women to build a powerful movement to sweep the guns and violence and poverty and poor education and drugs out of our homes and communities and replace them with hope and good schools, strong families and safe communities and a decent life for all children. It's time to act on Dr. Mary McLeod Bethune's advice to "stop playing bridge and start building bridges."

It will be very hard.

Black women face a multiple challenge of not being taken seriously by many White men, White women, Black men, and even other Black women, and by the White male-dominated media. White men in power often do not consider something to be credible or important until a White man says or does it. When I returned from Hanoi as a member of the Woodcock Commission appointed by President Carter to seek information about and the return of any Americans missing in action, I went on the "MacNeil/Lehrer NewsHour" to report on our trip, accompanied by a senior Defense Department official. I always over-prepare, particularly when studying a new issue, and was able to answer a question about the number and percentage of Americans missing in action in the Vietnam War compared to previous wars. Although the Defense official neither knew nor gave the answer, I was surprised when the written transcript of the show was shared with me by a friend to see that it attributed my answer to him. A brilliant senior Black woman foundation executive recounted how a White woman subordinate had asked not to report to her but rather directly to the White male foundation head so as not to lose her self-perceived status.

My greatest social peeve is reserved for White men who stand when White women enter the room and who do not stand when Black women enter the room. It is all right with me in this era of confused etiquette and of feminism if men do not stand or hold the door for any woman but it is not all right when they relay a message of unequal respect.

A very dear friend recounts how she learned the southern code of racial hypocrisy which so disturbed her. As a child she had been taught always to wait her turn in line. One day her mother stopped their car in front of the post office and told her to run inside and get a stamp to mail a letter. She got in line behind several Black women who had preceded her. When she returned to the car her mother impatiently demanded to know what had taken her so long. When she explained her mother replied that she had to wait her turn only when among White people.

Women are the backbone of the Black church without whom it would crumble. As in the Civil Rights Movement, Black women in the church are often asked and expected to take a back seat to the men who depend on but disempower them. An old friend who is a prominent Black Washington lawyer with whom I sometimes share great sermons and discuss great preachers astounded me not long ago by proclaiming that he and a leading Black preacher "do not like women preachers" after I had promised to send him sermons by two great women preachers I'd recently heard at the Alex Haley Farm. I could only relay my shock when I realized he was serious: "What kind of stupid backwards statement is that—and in 1998!"

He spontaneously revealed an attitude that too many men still hold, regarding women as instruments of their desires and needs and not as human beings of equal status due equal respect and opportunity. This powerful Black man is a reflection of the broader male societal disrespect for Black women and for women in general. When one speaks of shared power, shared parenting, shared responsibilities of husbands and wives in so many realms, men bristle and feel attacked. They often are unwilling to share power or control or to understand that a woman affirming herself is not disaffirming them.

Over the years I have been profoundly inspired by great women of all races who broke out of society's boxes, found and raised their powerful voices, took risks, and sacrificed all as they sought to be God's hands and feet on earth in a variety of ways. From Saint Clare, Saint Francis's friend and fellow seeker, to Saint Theresa of Avila to Dorothy Day to Eleanor Roosevelt to her friend Mary McLeod Bethune and Marian Anderson, these women like so many others courageously used God's gifts to lift themselves above manmade obstacles and to help transform their times. It is time, sisters of every race, class, faith, and place, to come together and build a new third millennial world fit for and worthy of our children.

⊰ 13 ⊱
OUR CHILDREN
AS MENTORS

I have learned many things from my teachers; I have learned many things from my friends; and I have learned even more from my students.

The Talmud

At that time Jesus said, I thank you, Father, Lord of heaven and earth, because you have hidden these things from the wise and the intelligent and have revealed them to infants.

Matthew 11:25–26

Children come into the world trusting until they are taught to distrust by adults who cannot be trusted.

Children come into the world without hate and racial prejudice until they are taught by adults who hate and are prejudiced.

Children come into the world resilient and full of joy and laughter until they are discouraged, demeaned, and stigmatized by the low expectations, unjust labels, and mistreatment of adults.

Children come into the world with promise and potential until they are pampered into laziness, purposelessness, and a sense of entitlement by too much wealth and too little challenge or trapped into failure by too much hunger, loneliness, poverty, and illiteracy.

Children come into the world with God's commission to live and learn and sing and dance and grow, then too many are decommissioned by adults who prey on, neglect, abuse, exploit, disrespect, discourage, and mislead them.

Children come into the world as God's gifts of life and love yet so many are spurned and not spared the ravages of war and gun violence that murder and maim and corrode their dreams and self-esteem.

"The human child," Nobel Peace laureate Alva Myrdal said, "is the greatest miracle of creation. Every single child . . . is a world of subtle secrets, a personality, a unique occurrence, never to be repeated on this earth." Yet our world and nation too often undermine these individual miracles by words and deeds that divide rather than bring children together and make every child feel that he or she belongs.

In our nation and world, White children have been assigned more value as a group than Black and Brown and Asian and Native American children. Affluent children are accorded more respect and resources than children who are poor and need them more. Children in single-parent families or born to teen parents are assigned the stigma we often attach to the parents they did not choose. Children with special physical, mental, or emotional needs are sometimes shunned and made the butt of jokes and jeers. Girls as a group face many barriers that boys do not in a world still characterized more by male privilege than by gender equality and mutual respect. Some boys—especially Black boys—are accorded no respect and are expected to control their rage from unequal treatment without crying or protesting—legally or illegally. And most boys are imprisoned by "male values" that teach that strong men don't cry and that life is a contest between winners and losers rather than between winners and winners and a struggle between self and God.

Children, because they are the primary responsibility of the parents who bring them into the world and are dependent on adults not only in their homes, but in their schools, communities, states, and nation to care for and prepare them for adulthood, are assigned a lesser social and political status than adults. Because they do not vote, lobby, contribute to political action committees, or hold press conferences, and lack powerful self-interested membership organizations, their needs often come last in public and private investment and attention. How else can we explain the fact that every sixty-six-year-old is accorded health care but every six- or sixteen-year-old is not? We provide Social Security to every senior citizen and deny the social security of basic nutrition, shelter, health care, and quality childhood education to young children in the crucial early years of life when their brains are developing at a rapid pace.

Toni Morrison, the 1989 Nobel laureate for literature, said in 1984 that, "Everywhere, everywhere, children are the scorned people of the Earth." Yet our children, God's gifts of hope and immortality, will inherit everything we have and are, and carry on—or not carry on—our values and institutions in the world to come. If we do not prepare them now for these responsibilities they will become our moral and economic Achilles heels who will trip and land America on its face rather than standing tall on its feet in the next century.

I do not think children can do no wrong. They will do wrong all the time if they are not lovingly cared for, taught right, and disciplined by caring and disciplined adults. I do not think that children's rude or violent conduct should be ignored or condoned any more than I think the rude and violent adults they often are emulating in real life or on the movie, television, and video screens from whom they learn their values—or lack of them—should be ignored or condoned. I believe youth and adult violence and crime should be swiftly and fairly punished. I also believe as numerous police chiefs do that it is best to prevent crime before it becomes necessary to punish it.

Our children already have served as the transforming catalysts for America's greatest moral movement of the twentieth century. Taylor Branch, Pulitzer Prize–winning author of *Parting the Waters* and *Pillar of Fire* said at a CDF/BCCC forum on Race, Children, and Poverty at the Memphis Civil Rights Museum where Dr. King was slain thirty years ago: "There is no precedent that I know of in recorded history for the power balance of a great nation turning on the moral witness of schoolchildren. This [civil rights] movement was steeped in the blood and the witness of children up through Selma." Taylor then said: "A movement that rode through in history on the spirit of children now looks to how we treat our children thirty years later. Now we have adults who, in effect, need to pay back children. I think the adult generation is going to be measured by how we treat it. If you look around, almost every single major American issue that needs to be addressed is around the way we treat our children. Whether it's schools, whether it's jails, whether it's cities, whether it's even the debt and the deficit, whether it's health. What are we going to leave our children? It's the major issue."

Just as youth demonstrated for civil rights, young people demonstrated against the Vietnam War and helped bring it to an end.

Our children offer the best opportunity to save ourselves, our country, our world, and our souls. Although adults have primary responsibility for safeguarding the lives and hopes of children and youths, young people need to feel and be empowered to advocate for themselves and others with adults as I and so many of my generation were empowered by the mentors in this memoir. Caring committed adult leadership coupled with a healthy respect for and guidance of youthful energy, intelligence, and creativity can empower a young person to act forcefully and successfully on behalf of a principle, others, and themselves. Children learn so much from adults but also have so much to teach us.

*CHILDREN HAVE TAUGHT ME TO CONFRONT UNVAR-
NISHED TRUTH AND UNPLEASANT FACTS I'D OFTEN LIKE
TO AVOID.* The day after Dr. King was shot, I went out into the riot-torn Washington, D.C. streets and into schools in those neighborhoods scorched by flames to talk to children. I went to tell them not to loot and riot so that they would not get arrested and ruin their futures. A young Black boy about twelve or thirteen years old looked squarely at me and said, "Lady, what future? I ain't got no future. I ain't got nothing to lose."

I've spent thirty years and will spend the rest of my life trying to prove him wrong. I had no idea how hard it would be. For this child saw and spoke the plain truth for himself and millions like him in our money rich, militarily powerful, but morally anemic, race-, gender-, and income-stratified society. I'm pleased that millions of Black and poor children have received a Head Start, child care, health care, immunizations, and a better education. But millions are still left behind. Despite great progress over the past thirty years, so much peril remains to snuff out the hopes and dreams and lives of millions of children like him. A Black child is still twice as likely as a White child to die in the first year of life, three times as likely to live in extreme poverty, and four times as likely to be a homicide victim as a teenager.

❧ CHILDREN HAVE TAUGHT ME FORGIVENESS. How often I have hurt my children intentionally and unintentionally with harsh words, impatient actions, inattention in times of need, unfair judgments, too much emphasis on their mistakes rather than their achievements, and trying to make them live my dreams rather than helping them live and realize their own dreams. I've so appreciated them (often later) telling me when I am or was wrong but loving me still. So many children whose parents abuse and violate them in unspeakable ways still loyally cling to them, giving the parents the love they themselves seek so desperately from those who brought them into the world. Too often we adults cannot forgive ourselves or others or are debilitated by the corrosive weight of old grudges and prejudices.

❧ CHILDREN HAVE TAUGHT ME RESILIENCY. What parent has not marveled at how quickly children can snap back from a high fever or illness and return to his or her active duty of play? I have watched with wonder and gratitude the silent and depressed children, alcohol or cocaine addicted at birth, rise from the dead to life through the love of adoptive and foster parents. As I have watched some of these children adopted by CDF staff and family members blossom, it increases my sense of the urgency of our child advocacy work to grab as much life and hope as possible from the ruins.

Every year the Children's Defense Fund and local groups honor five youths in about a dozen cities who are "Beating the Odds." They represent hundreds of thousands of similar youths whom we do not see and hear about but who are getting up every day and climbing over obstacles stacked against them by broken families, homelessness, violence, and drug-ridden homes, schools, and neighborhoods. Children like Marino Angulo, one of our first "Beat the Odds" youths, who kept his whole family together when his mother went to prison and his father, plagued by alcohol, abandoned the family for several years. He kept going to school and kept helping his younger sisters and brothers with their homework while doing his. He worked to help support them and with the help of a caring teacher managed to get into and finish college. Now a teacher himself after graduating from Whittier College, his example has inspired his younger brothers and sisters to try to emulate his success.

‣ CHILDREN HAVE TAUGHT ME WONDER AND TO SEE THE WORLD AFRESH EACH DAY. I loved traveling with my sons (before adolescence!), when their first reaction to new places and people was *look, look, oooh,* or *that's neat,* or *that's cool.* Rachel Carson, author of the great book *Silent Spring,* said, "A child's world is fresh and new and beautiful, full of wonder and excitement. It is our misfortune that for most of us that clear-eyed vision, that true instinct for what is beautiful and awe-inspiring, is dimmed and even lost before we reach adulthood."

‣ CHILDREN TEACH US THAT LOVE MATTERS MOST. Anthony Williams was born at Los Angeles General Hospital to a teen mother who was unable to care for him. He was placed in foster care where he was left to lie in his crib for many lonely hours with no one talking, reading, or singing to him or turning him over in his crib. As a result, he later required corrective surgery on his ear and tongue from such long periods of lying on one side. Silent and thought to be retarded, he was on the verge of being placed in an institution.

Someone aware of Anthony's condition urged the Williams family to consider adopting him before he was institutionalized. Mr. Williams felt his family's resources were already stretched to the limit with two children and another on the way. Mrs. Williams disagreed and nagged her husband until he relented if she could find the money required by the adoption process. She had trained as an opera singer and got a bit part in "Carmen" to earn enough to adopt.

Anthony, a child who had never spoken until Mrs. Virginia Williams and her husband took him in and loved him back to life, found his voice, confidence, and abilities in the Williams family which eventually grew to eight children including two additional adopted children. After some rough patches, Anthony went on to graduate from Yale College, Harvard Law School, and Harvard's Kennedy School of

Government. He is now Mayor of the District of Columbia. I believe there are thousands, even millions of children like little Anthony whose great potential is lost to America and the world by parental, community, and societal neglect.

⬦ CHILDREN TEACH US TO BE COURAGEOUS AND TO STAND UP AGAINST INJUSTICE. Dr. Robert Coles, in his children's book *The Story of Ruby Bridges,* describes Ruby's loving forgiveness and courage when faced with the ugly screaming White crowds who jeered and taunted her as she attended alone, only six years old, a previously all-White school in New Orleans boycotted by Whites. Ruby astonished her teacher when she asked Ruby why she had paused and talked to the crowd of White adults one day. "I wasn't talking," said Ruby. "I was praying. I was praying for them." Every morning Ruby said she stopped a few blocks away from school to say a prayer for the people who hated her. This morning she forgot until she was already in the middle of the angry mob. This is the prayer little Ruby told Robert Coles she repeated twice daily—before and after school:

> Please, God, try to forgive those people.
> Because even if they say those bad things,
> They don't know what they're doing.
> So you could forgive them.
> Just like You did those folks a long time ago
> When they said terrible things about you.

Taylor Branch in his books chronicling the Civil Rights Movement, and David Halberstam in *The Children,* recount the incredible courage and determination and grit of the children and youths who constituted many of the frontline soldiers in the often violent and always tough war to end discrimination in the American South. Their names were not just on the court papers filed by their brave parents in *Brown v. Board of Education, Cooper v. Aaron, Carter v. Drew Municipal School District*, and dozens of other school desegregation cases filed on their behalf by civil rights lawyers. Children like little Ruby were the shock troops who parted the waters of injustice Taylor Branch describes and weathered day after day the hateful isolation and ugly epithets encouraged or ignored by some White adults who taught their children to spurn and insult Black children. Children faced fierce police dogs and fire hoses and filled the jails in Birmingham and Selma, Alabama when so many adults hesitated out of fear for their jobs or personal safety. Children withstood arrests and rough treatment by policemen in Jackson, Mississippi and harsh treatment in southern jails where they were detained. High school and college youths sat down until lunch counters across the South were desegregated. Children suffered physical and emotional injuries when Whites shot indiscriminately through the windows of their homes or threatened them and their parents. Children were sometimes beaten by police for standing up for freedom. Four little girls had to die as a sacrifice in Birmingham before the nation assured Black citizens the right to vote that led to the election of many Black officials and more decent White elected officials from the South. Those officials—and all of us—owe children fair treatment, leadership, and protection today.

⊰ 14 ⊱
AMERICA AS MENTOR
FOR ITS CHILDREN AND
THE WORLD

Might it be that this land with all of its richness, with all of its opportunity for true greatness, its opportunity to present itself before the world as what a nation ought to be, might not be sowing the seeds of its very destruction in abandonment of its children?

Dr. Gardner Taylor, Pastor Emeritus,
Concord Baptist Church,
1996 sermon at Haley Farm

It is not the place we occupy which is important, but the direction in which we move.

Oliver Wendell Holmes

THE UNITED STATES is the sole superpower in the waning twentieth-century world. We stand first among industrialized countries in military technology, in military exports, in Gross Domestic Product, in the number of millionaires and billionaires, in health technology, and in defense expenditures. But we stand tenth in our children's eighth-grade science scores, sixteenth in living standards among our poorest one-fifth of children, seventeenth in low-birthweight rates, eighteenth in infant mortality, twenty-first in eighth-grade math scores, and last in protecting our children against gun violence.

In the United States we are reaping what we have sown in child neglect. A child is born into poverty every forty seconds, is reported abused or neglected every eleven seconds, runs away from home every twenty-four seconds, drops out of school every nine seconds of the school day. A child bears a child every minute. Our seeds of cultural violence, militarism, and senseless trafficking in guns have produced an alarming crop of firearm deaths and violence that stalks our children at school, at home, and in their neighborhoods and leaves no American safe.

God has blessed America with enormous wealth and power but how wisely are we using them? President Clinton is proposing to invest $1.5 trillion over the next five years to protect our children against purported enemies lurking outside our borders and Congress will try to spend far more. Yet not a single American child has been killed by guns at the hands of a Russian, Chinese, North Korean, African, Syrian, or Cuban citizen outside our borders, while thousands die from the guns in their own homes, schools, and neighborhoods every year.

President Clinton has proposed to splurge another $10.5 billion over the next five years for the so-called "Star Wars" national defense system that has flunked every test after ten years and $40 billion of taxpayer investment. "Star Wars" is over and above the $36.6 billion in planned costs for an alphabet-soup bowlful of defense systems (Patriot PAC3, THAAD, MEADS, AEGIS, two different laser beam weapons). Our children don't need protection in the stars; they need protection in their schools and communities from bullets and drugs and from the ignorance, sickness, poverty, hunger, and homelessness that are killing them more slowly but as surely. Political analyst William Greider estimated recently that it costs $2,000 an hour to operate an M-1 tank. That's $48,000 a day. That money would serve about 5,800 more children in after-school programs or provide 2,900 more women and babies adequate nutrition through the effective WIC program. Which do you feel is a better investment for a more secure America?

Although the United States is getting richer its children are remaining poor. Between 1969 and 1997 the number of poor children grew by 46 percent (more than 4 million). Seventy percent of all poor American children live in a household where someone works. And more White children are poor than Black or Brown children. While our economy was changing, rising economic inequality drove up the percentage of workers below poverty level and the already meager safety net for children lost more ground in the 1980s. The elderly saw their poverty rate plunge in half. If the safety net was as effective at lifting low-income children as low-income elderly out of poverty, three out of four of today's poor children would not be poor. If the safety net for American children was as effective as it is in Great Britain, three out of five of our poor children would not be poor.

Demographics show that by 2030 non-White children will constitute a majority of American children. Their fate will help shape America's future as much as White children. Yet racism, hate crimes, police brutality, and backlash against equitable measures to help inner-city schools and minorities overcome past and present inequality are resurging across America. Painful past lessons about the high social and human costs of racial inequality are forgotten as some political leaders, more interested in sound bites than sound policy and in appealing to our worst rather than our better natures, lead us to oppose measures that work for children and that will benefit all Americans and ensure a productive future work force. The wonderful southern writer Lillian Smith believed that

> Delinquency is tied up so closely with the hate talk and with racial arrogance and racial shame. If we could convince the people of Georgia that Talmadge is waging warfare against the emotional growth of children, we could get new allies on our side. Most white people do not think they and their children are harmed by racial discrimination. They think if they work for racial democracy, that they are working for Negroes. Our job is to convince them that they are working for themselves and their children's future.

Former Treasury Secretary Robert Rubin told 1998 Harvard Business School graduates that a respected European magazine interviewer predicted that although the U.S. economy was currently very strong, in fifteen or twenty years it would be a second-tier economy for two reasons: our public schools and our inner cities. Rubin told the graduates: "In many ways he was right. These are the challenges that we must meet if we are going to be productive and competitive in the global economy in the years and decades ahead."

◆

If I could be granted one wish and pass one universal law, I would dramatically decrease the arsenals of nuclear and conventional weapons of death in the world and invest the hundreds of billions of saved resources in tools of life for the hungry, homeless, sick, and uneducated children and people at home and around the globe. It would cost an estimated $62 billion to lift every American child out of poverty by providing jobs, child care, and supplementing below-poverty parental earnings. That is how much we spend every eighty-two days on the military and less than a third of the estimated increase in our Gross Domestic Product in 2000.

It would take between $7,000 and $10,000 *a year* to provide quality child care and a Head Start to help get every child ready for school. That's what we spend *an hour* on long-range military flights to foreign countries and what we spend *every two seconds* on federal welfare for wealthy corporations.

What can each of us do to change our nation's priorities and build decent and safe communities for every child?

▶ FIRST: *EVERY ADULT can take responsibility for protecting children and for discouraging violence and racial and any intolerance as family and national values.* I believe strongly that all adults have a responsibility to do no harm and to protect children. I believe parents ought to teach children right from wrong, to keep them as physically, mentally, emotionally, and morally secure as possible, and to set limits (which every child and teen sees as his or her job to test). However, no parent raises a child alone. No parent can control the violence so embedded in our psyches and culture waiting to burst forth at any time from the ubiquitous rage lethalized by over 200 million guns in circulation all over America. No parent alone can protect children from polluted food, air, airwaves, water, and a depleted ozone layer. No parent alone can protect a child completely from the relentless and addictive materialistic messages of our consumer society or from the smut on the Internet, television, or movie screens.

Never have we seen such incessant and crass marketing of violence, addictive substances, incivility, and material things to children as consumers. What values beyond money would lead anyone to produce games for the young called "You Are Going to Die" or "Doom" that portray killing as fun and desensitize children to cruelty and violence? How many of the producers or actors or underwriters of movies saturated with gratuitous violence would want their own children and grandchildren to see them? How many toy manufacturers think or care about whether their toys might encourage aggression? How many television leaders, writers, producers, stars, and advertisers think about the quality and content of their programming and whether it might have a harmful impact on young vulnerable minds?

The average child has watched 5,478 hours of television by age five, the equivalent of $7\frac{1}{2}$ months of twenty-four-hour days or fifteen months of twelve-hour days. Children spend more time watching television than doing homework and reading combined. The lines between make-believe and real life blur in some children's rudderless lives unpeopled by enough caring adults transmitting positive values or helping them interpret what they see. Should it surprise us that a small percentage of alienated children carry out their fantasies about guns and violence in real life? Is it enough to tell parents to turn off the television set and carefully monitor the time and the shows their children watch? (Parents should!) Since a plethora of studies show that violent television is a risk factor that contributes to real violence, why would those who create violent shows hide behind the First Amendment to cover up their irresponsibility in caring for children and public safety?

We all must put children at the center of our family and community lives. Employers and government at all levels must ask whether their policies and practices—from wages to health insurance to child care to parental leave and flex-time to volunteer opportunities—make it easier or harder for parents to meet their children's needs and to balance work and family responsibilities. Educators must put children at the center of schools and be held accountable for teaching children to read, write, and learn math and science at grade level. Cultural leaders must rely more on creativity than on gore. Faith communities, schools, and other community institutions must engage with and connect children and youths to useful, purposeful, interesting service and action opportunities so that another generation of disengaged cynical citizens will not spell the death knell of American civic and spiritual life.

We must act now to take guns out of the hands of children and those who kill children. Whether you are a hunter, NRA member, gun owner or not I hope you will agree that each citizen must do everything we can to prevent children from killing and being killed by guns. We all must join in working for responsible regulation of guns. An overwhelming majority of Americans favor gun control measures, including over 80 percent of gun owners. I hope voters, especially women voters, will insist that our leaders protect our children instead of guns. I hope they will hold coffee klatches, study groups, and prayer circles to study the facts about gun violence and children, the myths about the Second Amendment, and what can be done to keep our children safe.

⊱ SECOND, IT IS TIME *for all adults to stop our hypocrisy and double standards.* Children need consistent adult guidance and moral example in their homes, congregations, schools, public life, media, and culture. We do not have a child and youth problem in our nation; we have an adult problem that we must confront if we are to put our children on a healthy and safe course. Adults must stop blaming children for acting out lessons we adults teach or have left children to figure out on their own from our overt and covert personal, professional, and cultural signals. And we adults should stop fingerpointing and blaming each other about who is causing the child neglect, youth violence, and alienation so evident in our schools and in every strata of American society. We all are responsible.

Our children see us adults preach one thing and practice another. Today two out of every three Black and one-fifth of all White babies are born to never-married mothers. If it's wrong for thirteen-year-old inner-city girls to have babies without the benefit of marriage, it's wrong for rich celebrities and we ought to stop putting them on the cover of *People* magazine. If it is wrong for teens and children to abuse, bully, ridicule, and torment other children (and it is), then it is wrong for adults in the home, workplace, and political life to do so. It is adults who have engaged in epidemic abuse of children and of each other in our homes. It is adults who have taught children to kill and disrespect human life. It is adults who manufacture, market, and profit from the guns that have turned many neighborhoods and schools into war zones and the blood of children into profits.

It is adults who have financed, produced, directed, and starred in the movies, television shows, and music that have made graphic violence ubiquitous in our culture. It is adults who have borne children and then left millions of them behind and alone without enough love and attention or moral guidance and millions more without basic health care, shelter, or food. It is adults who have taught our children to look for meaning outside rather than inside themselves, teaching them, in Dr. King's words, "to judge success by the index of our salaries or the size of our automobiles, rather than by the quality of our service and relationship to humanity." It is adults who have passed on the poisons of racism and intolerance from generation to generation. And it is adults who have to stand up and be adults, examine our lives and values, and accept our responsibility to parent and protect the young.

⋫ THIRD: WE CAN AFFIRM *the individual worth and special strengths of each child and stop squeezing children into adult bureaucratic categories and boxes that stifle youthful creativity and potential.* I love a parable I read first in a book by Dr. Howard Thurman and later in an Outward Bound Reader: "Once upon a time, the animals decided they must do something heroic to meet the problems of a 'new world.' So they organized a school. They adopted an activity curriculum consisting of running, climbing, swimming and flying. To make it easier to administer the curriculum, *all* the animals took *all* the subjects. The duck was excellent in swimming, in fact better than his instructor, but he made only passing grades in flying and was very poor in running. Since he was slow in running, he had to stay after school and also drop swimming in order to practice running. This was kept up until his web feet were badly worn and he was only average in swimming. But average was acceptable in school, so nobody worried about that except the duck. The rabbit started at the top of the class in running, but had a nervous breakdown because of so much make-up work in swimming. The squirrel was excellent in climbing until he developed frustration in the flying class, where his teacher made him start from the ground up instead of from the treetop down. He also developed 'charlie horses' from overexertion and got C in climbing and D in running. The eagle was a problem child and was disciplined severely. In the climbing class he beat all the others to the top of the tree, but insisted on using his own way to get there. At the end of the year an abnormal eel that could swim exceedingly well, and also run, climb, and fly a little, had the highest average and was valedictorian. The prairie dogs stayed out of school and fought the tax levy because the administration would not add digging and burrowing to the curriculum. They apprenticed their child to a badger and later joined the groundhog and gophers to start a successful private school."

Education reform is again at the forefront of public concern. As the last election of the twentieth century looms, politicians' lips drip with talk about the need to teach our children to read and to reform our schools. But we have heard this song before when President Bush and all fifty governors, led by then governor Clinton of Arkansas, adopted achievable and important goals for the education of all of America's children by the year 2000. Not a single one of the goals will be met including the cornerstone goal of getting every child ready for school. Round two of education reform must not be rhetorical; it must be real or children and the nation will lose profoundly.

Too often lost in talk about education "reform" is the simple fact that education is about one thing—children—whose needs must come first. Education is not about adult jobs or political interests or convenience. It is about preparing every child to become a confident, competent citizen. America's public education system—the pillar of our democracy—needs revitalization and refocusing on the well-being of *all* students. A deep sense of urgency is necessary to face the challenge of preparing a new generation of children for the future.

🙖 FOURTH: *IT IS TIME for America to be fair to children and accord them the respect and priority worthy of a just, sensible, compassionate society.* Is it fair that no school system of any size with any diversity of children has ever educated the vast majority or all of its children to high levels of achievement?

Is it fair that poor children in the poorest neighborhoods have the poorest schools, the poorest prepared teachers, the poorest equipment, the poorest school buildings, libraries, laboratories, the fewest computers, counselors, school nurses, and enrichment programs, and the lowest expectations by teachers and a public that blame them for achieving poorly on the tests for which we have not prepared them?

Is it fair that hard-working citizens who mold the future by caring for children are the least well-paid in our society? Is a full-time early-childhood educator whose median earnings in 1998 were $265 a week, about $13,250 a year with no health benefits, worth less to the community than a car-wash attendant who earned 20 percent more? Is a good elementary school teacher who earns $34,550 a year with some benefits really worth only three hours and twenty minutes of a $20.5 million annual compensation package for a CEO whose company produces cigarettes that addict millions of children and kill millions of human beings? Should a hairdresser or manicurist have required hours of training when a child care worker in many states has none?

Is it fair that corporations drain tens of billions of taxpayer dollars every year in corporate welfare and special tax breaks while we have cut billions from safety net programs for children and poor families? Shamefully over six million poor children lived in families with incomes of less than half the poverty line of $6,401 for a family of three. That's less than the military will spend *each second* if the Clinton administration's budget proposals prevail and less than *one hour* of the compensation of the cigarette company CEO. Is it fair that senior citizens have a health and income safety net and children do not?

🙖 FIFTH: *HELP BUILD a powerful movement to protect and Leave No Child Behind, and ensure all children a Healthy Start, a Head Start, a Fair Start, a Safe Start, and a Moral Start and successful passage to adulthood with the help of caring families and communities.* America

should lead not lag the world on key child indicators and on funda-
mental human rights and justice for children just as we now lead on
military and monetary indexes. Countless youths in inner-city neighborhoods are imprisoned by poverty and lack of skills where "the future" means surviving the day and where living to eighteen is a tri-
umph. And countless non-poor youths are imprisoned by affluenza—
too many things with too little meaning—unaware that life is more
than material goods or thrills that do not satisfy. They share a common deeper hunger for a food that fills their souls. Their neglect and
marginalization by parents, schools, communities, and our nation
turned them first to and then against each other in gangs and then
against a society that would rather demonize, imprison, market to
and profit from rather than educate, employ, and empower them. Our
market culture tells poor children they must have designer sneakers,
gold chains, and fancy cars to be somebody while denying them the
jobs to buy them legally. Our rich children have these things but find
them no substitute for love, attention, and purpose beyond self. So
they are both easy marks for drug and gun dealers who hawk their
harmful products to our young. Isn't it time to commit to respecting
children's basic human rights affirmed in the Universal Declaration of
Human Rights signed fifty years ago by many of the nations of the
world with the leadership of Eleanor Roosevelt? Isn't it time for the
U.S. to end the disgrace of being the only legally constituted government in the world that has not ratified the Convention on the Rights
of the Child? Why should the U.S. not subscribe to the principle of
protecting children? With U.S. ratification, this nonbinding commitment to children can become the first universally ascribed human
rights treaty in the world and become a standard we and all nations of
the world seek to and can achieve in the twenty-first century.

•

Women, especially mothers and grandmothers, must be key catalysts
in protecting children in the next era. Slave woman Sojourner Truth
gave us our charge when she said: "If the first woman God ever made
was strong enough to turn the world upside down all alone, these
women together ought to be able to turn it back, and get it right side

up again." We must speak up and organize against war and violence, poverty and illiteracy and intolerance at home and abroad. While men have to be full partners, it is time for women to lead the way in redefining national priorities, the meaning of success, and to leave an imperishable inheritance of activated compassion and love to our children.

We are living at an incredible moral moment in history. Few human beings are blessed to anticipate or experience the beginning of both a new century and millennium. How will we say thanks for the life, earth, nation, and children God has entrusted to our care? What principles will we stand for, practice, and send to the future through our children to their children and to a spiritually confused, balkanized, and violent nation and world desperately hungering for moral leadership?

How will progress be measured over the next thousand years if we survive them? By the kill power and number of our weapons, or by our willingness to shrink, indeed destroy, the nuclear and conventional arms prison we have constructed in the name of peace and security? Will we be remembered as one of the most violent nations in history or as the people who learned to relate to each other and to our world neighbors in nonviolent ways? Will America's legacy be how many material things we produce, advertise, sell, and consume, or our rediscovery of more lasting nonmaterial measures of success—a new Dow-Jones for the purpose and quality of life? Will we be remembered by how rapidly corporate merger mania can render human beings and human work obsolete, or by our efforts to ensure a better balance between corporate profits and corporate caring for children, families, and communities?

Will we be remembered for how much a few at the top can get at the expense of the many at the bottom and in the middle, or for our struggle for a concept of enough for all Americans and for the poor of the earth? Will we be remembered for the glitz, style, violence, and banality of much of our culture, or for the substance of our efforts to rekindle an ethic of caring, community, and justice in our world?

Can our founding principle "that all men are created equal" and "are endowed by their Creator with certain inalienable rights" withstand the test of time, the tempests of politics, and become deed and not just creed for every man, woman, and child? Is America's dream big enough for every second child who is female, every fifth child who is poor, every sixth child who is Black, every seventh child who is Latino, and every eighth child who is mentally or physically challenged?

Indian philosopher Rabindranath Tagore said that each child "comes with the message that God is not yet discouraged of man." I believe that our children can become the healing agents for our national and world transformation and that protecting children is the moral litmus test of our humanity and the overarching moral challenge in our nation and world.

AFTERWORD

A Parent's Pledge and Twenty-Five More Lessons for Life

WHEN MY OLDEST SON reached his twenty-first birthday, I wondered what I could give him at this important milestone that would have lasting value. I decided to write him a letter about his rich family heritage as a young Black man with a mixed racial and religious heritage trying to grow up in America.

I shared twenty-five lessons for life that I had been taught by my parents and elders which later formed the core of *The Measure of Our Success: A Letter to My Children and Yours*, for which my second son wrote the foreword. When my youngest son reached his twenty-first birthday, I began jotting down more lessons to share with him and his two brothers in a world that is ever more challenging. Like most young adults, they do not always welcome or follow parental lessons. But like most mothers, I keep sharing them anyway as lanterns of love I hope will lighten and enlighten their paths and that of their children and their children's children.

The overarching message of this book is not about what we *tell* our children; it is about what we adults do and value as parents, citizens, educators, religious, cultural, corporate, civic, and political leaders. It is about the need for adults to struggle to live what we preach, to say what we mean, to mean what we say, and to be what we seem. While parents have first and primary responsibility for their children, the ability to exercise that responsibility requires the support of *every* sector including government at every level. The National Conference of Catholic Bishops stated, "The undeniable fact is that our children's future is shaped both by the values of their parents and the policies of our nation."

Like all adults, I sometimes pretend, lie, and make mistakes that hurt my children and others, and offend every hour and day when I would not. I marvel at the forgiving spirit of my children ever so aware of my foibles and lapses in following my own advice. But I don't mind that they see my struggles as long as they also see that I can admit I was wrong and am earnestly trying to learn from my mistakes and do better. I hope our parents, teachers, preachers, citizens, and leaders will open our eyes and ears and shed our convenient ignorance and answer our children's calls for help.

Before I share any more lessons with young people, I want to share a pledge made with the hindsight wisdom of thirty years of parenting mistakes and successes which I hope parents and all adults will take to protect and care for children.

In several 1953 sermons to various South Carolina audiences on "Citizenship Education for a Period of Transition," my daddy, a Baptist minister, said the following which seems so apt today.

> The necessary qualification of parents for today's children may be largely determined by the total impact of our shrinking transitory world. Ours is an age of international citizenship. The environment of the children today is beset with divided loyalties and tragic woes of split personalities. And in their honest efforts to be realistic, to make sense of this wholesale adult insanity, they are almost dumbfounded so that argument becomes trivial. They are being flanked on all sides by the whirlwinds of contradictions that do not make sense.
>
> What then must need be the qualification of parents of today's children?
>
> I think parents ought to make every possible effort to keep an awareness of the transitions and the pressures of the times through which our children are called on to pass and be able to note with deep appreciation their power in personality changes of our children.
>
> Parents need to be qualified to give to the children of today moral discipline and spiritual poise so that they can weather the storm of periods of transition. It is ours as parents and children to live in a time of strange

irony suggesting the urgency of parents staking down the faith of their children in God and thus developing in them their moral and religious values, thereby preparing them for intelligent, effective, and loyal participation in the life of the family, community, the nation, and for world citizenship.

We must not tear down before we build up the children of today. Parents for today's children must at all cost provide a home, center of love for the nurture and security of their children who are sorely affected by the conduct of parents. Like parent, like child is a true proverb that makes parental responsibility sacred.

Above all, parents are duty bound to keep their home intact for the sake of children. If romance and happiness leave, then you must settle for duty. Nothing must separate parents from duty. The child first and always a center of love you owe. The tragedy of our civilization is the increasing number of broken homes.

Please join me in pledging allegiance to our children and grandchildren, to their growth, their safety, their well-being, and their futures.

I PLEDGE TO:

❧ *LISTEN TO MY CHILDREN.* Take time and really HEAR them. Look them in the eye and feel what they're saying even when they're searching for the words to express what they don't yet understand. Listen between the lines for their emotions. Let them know you're always there with an open ear, heart, and mind. Listening does not require you to agree with all they want; it means hearing what they feel they need.

❧ *COMMUNICATE WITH MY CHILDREN.* Ask them hard questions even when you think you can't do it. Get into their business. They won't like it but it's your responsibility. Tell them the truth, even when it's the hardest thing in the world to do. Talk with them about sex, drugs, violence, and crime and keep the lines of communication open. Talk with them about your family history, the culture of your people, and the legacy of overcoming any obstacles in your path.

♭ TEACH MY CHILDREN RIGHT FROM WRONG AND BE A GOOD ROLE MODEL FOR THEM. In a world where our values have been so perverted, it is our responsibility to chart and lead a course toward a higher moral ground. And since our children pay far more attention to our actions than to our words, we must struggle to practice what we preach.

♭ SPEND TIME WITH AND PAY ATTENTION TO MY CHILDREN. This isn't easy in today's world. With the competing demands of work, family, and day-to-day survival we're often racing the clock. But we've got to create opportunities to focus on and make our children the center of our attention. It doesn't cost money or require any special tools. Read to your children and have them read to you. Make up poems and songs, draw pictures, take photographs, play games together. Your children don't need the latest toys or technology as much as they need your attention. Let them know how important they are to you.

♭ EDUCATE MY CHILDREN IN MIND, BODY, AND SOUL. Our children's education doesn't begin and end at school. Surveys reveal that young people consistently rate their parents as their greatest heroes and role models. As their first and most significant teachers, parents have the obligation and the opportunity to set the stage for lifelong learning. Monitor and limit their TV, movie, and Internet viewing, and when you do watch TV, try to do it together and use what you see to teach. Eat and feed them a healthy diet and encourage exercise. Ask them to teach you the latest dance steps. And remember their spiritual development. Whether or not you attend church or temple or mosque regularly, talk with your children about the need to respect others and the Earth we share. Give them a sense of faith and hope and respect for a power greater than themselves.

❧ Work to provide a stable family life for my children. Families come in many shapes and sizes today and stability is one of the most important factors in a child's well-being. Keep as much continuity in children's lives as possible, and if and when change comes, think first about their needs and teach them to cope with it in positive, healthy ways. Let them know that you will always be there for them no matter what life may bring, and that they are not responsible for your adult problems. Talk with your children about their losses and fears and let them know you are available. Pray for and see the good in them even at moments when it isn't visible to the naked eye. And see the value in all children and remember them in your prayers as well.

❧ Vote for my children to ensure them fair treatment and opportunity. Children can't vote, but parents and grandparents can. We must keep children's needs in mind when supporting and selecting our political leaders. Pay attention to what candidates and representatives *do* on behalf of children. Call, visit, write and e-mail them to remind them that you're watching. Teach your children that their ancestors fought and died for the right to vote and that it is a powerful tool of citizenship. Take your children to vote with you and vote for candidates who vote for a strong children's agenda. Insist that whoever you vote for commits to investing in measures that work to assure all children a Healthy Start, a Head Start, a Fair Start, and a Safe Start in life and positive youth development. Request CDF's annual agenda, reports, and voting records on how fairly our leaders are treating children and how you can help.

❧ Speak out and stand up for my children's needs and support effective groups that help children. You are your child's greatest advocate. Use your power to speak and act on their behalf. Our children and families are facing one of the worst crises in American history and we've got to do something about it. Our voices united in concern can make a mighty roar. And by supporting effective groups, we build a stronger foundation for every child's and our own future. Stand For Children every year on or around June first in every state. Contact www.stand.org.

TWENTY-FIVE MORE LESSONS FOR LIFE

༄ LESSON 1: *Always remember that you are God's child. No man or woman can look down on you and you cannot look down on any man or woman or child.* Booker T. Washington recounted a conversation he had with Frederick Douglass who shared an unpleasant racial incident. While traveling in Pennsylvania, Douglass was forced to ride in a baggage car although he had paid the same price for his ticket as White passengers. Some White passengers who saw what happened went into the baggage car to express their sorrow that he had been degraded in this manner. Mr. Douglass straightened himself up on the box where he was sitting and replied: "They cannot degrade Frederick Douglass. The soul that is within me no man can degrade. I am not the one that is being degraded on account of this treatment, but those who are inflicting it upon me."

Theologian Howard Thurman's grandmother recounted to him how her slave preacher repeatedly reminded his slave congregation: "You—you are not niggers. You—you are not slaves. You are God's children." I hope every child of color in this nation and world will internalize this message. I also hope every "geek" and lonely and alienated child scarred by insensitive adults and peers will too. Adults who teach children to devalue themselves or to mistreat other children deserve pity and correction. Only when enough adults practice and teach children love and respect at home, in schools, religious congregations, and in our political and civic life will racial, gender, and religious intolerance and hate crimes subside in America and the world.

༄ LESSON 2: *Don't wait for, expect, or rely on favors. Count on earning them by hard work and perseverance.* So many of us try to get by on who we know rather than what we know and work hard and long to achieve. If you rely on who you know, those who give can also take away. In no way do I seek to disparage networking and support groups. Who has not benefited from sharing experiences with those who struggled and succeeded in similar circumstances and from being lent a helping hand? And yet who among us has not seen or experienced how the "old boy" networks of elites have often profited at the expense of excluded women, minority groups, and poor people? I hope when more women and minorities crack the glass ceilings of powerful White male privilege, they will not simply join the club but help transform it. Be grateful for good breaks and kind favors but don't count on them.

LESSON 3: *Call things by their right names.* We live in a culture riddled with hypocrisy. Advertising manufactures new needs and desires, makes us believe products are better than they are, and often uses symbols and slogans to deceive and mislead. The MX missile, a mass killer, is called a peacemaker, "The Marlboro Man" lures wannabe ruggeds to their death, and Joe Camel's hip pose sucked thousands of children into tobacco addiction. The NRA's "Eddie Eagle," Joe Camel's equivalent for guns, is designed more to hook children on shooting guns than on gun safety. Gun manufacturers market pearl-handled handguns to mothers as baby protectors although more children and adults are killed from guns in their households than by criminals on the streets. Political spin often trivializes and misleads. Mike McCurry, President Clinton's former press secretary, referred to the Administration's complete dismantlement of the sixty-year-old income safety net for poor mothers and children as "trimmings of the edges."

LESSON 4: *Don't listen to naysayers offering no solutions or take* no *or* but *for an answer.* Michael Henderson in *The Forgiveness Factor: Stories of Hope in a World of Conflict* tells the story of a famous evangelist confronted by a critic saying: "I don't like your way of doing things." The evangelist replied, "I am not very satisfied with them myself. How do you do it?" "Oh, I don't do that sort of thing," the critic responded. "In that case," the evangelist said, "I prefer my way of doing it to your way of not doing it." A lot of people come up to me after speeches saying how much they support CDF's goals for children but simply do not support our strategies or this particular strategy. When I ask them how they would meet children's needs in better ways, the most frequent answer is: "I don't know." How many times have I heard, especially from politicians, "I am for children *but* it will take more time to get done; *but* I don't like this particular proposal; *but* this is not the right time; *but* you need to build the political support for it and come back; *but* the other party will block it." "I want children to get health coverage *but* we ought to cover their parents too (I agree); *but* we need to balance the budget and there is no money to cover parents or all children; *but* I'm against a new government program." I've learned to answer these and other *buts* with my own *buts*: "*But* just do it because children are dying every day and that's morally wrong and unnecessary. *But* there are many ways to provide health coverage for children building on existing successful private sector and governmental models. *But* we can pay for it in the same way Congress pays for military increases and capital gains tax breaks and corporate welfare. *But* immunizing children and preventing emergency room care saves money."

☞ LESSON 5: *Don't be afraid to stick your neck out, to make mistakes, or to speak up.* Not stupid, careless mistakes that can result in AIDS or death or that can hurt yourself and others, or mistakes you've already made and know their harmful consequences. I mean mistakes that come from trying to make a difference. In one of his sermons my father spoke of a picture of a turtle with its neck stuck out in the office of former Harvard President Conant which had the caption: "I can't go forward if I don't stick my neck out." Mahatma Gandhi wrote to a friend, "Speak the truth, without fear and without exception. You are in God's work, so you need not fear man's scorn. If they listen to your requests and grant them, you will be satisfied. If they reject them, then you must make their rejection your strength." The late Rev. Walter Murray, the gentle but courageous Lynn, Massachusetts religious leader who, after the shooting death of a youth, helped achieve safe parks and community patrols by confronting city leaders who claimed they had no money for such things, asked in a Haley Farm sermon, "Why it is that all of us who preach and sing about our powerful Father God on Sunday are afraid to confront people in power on Monday? Why is it that men of God forget who they serve in the face of earthly power and prestige?"

┦ LESSON 6: *Keep your word and your commitments.* If you get married, stay married. Your children need stability and marriage is not to be shed lightly like old clothes. While I do not condone tolerating domestic violence or conditions where it is unsafe for a spouse or child to remain in a family, I also do not believe that simply seeking personal happiness or fulfillment should come at the expense of a child's home and well-being. Who among us has not been bored, angry, disappointed, or eager for a more exciting and fulfilling spouse —sentiments I'm sure our spouses have shared. But a family is more than the desires of one or both adults. Children should come first.

┦ LESSON 7: *Be strategic, focus, and don't scatter your energies on many things that don't add up to a better whole.* Put yourself in the other person's shoes and figure out how what you want will benefit them and not just you. So many advocates for children and the poor are ineffective because we spend more time on what we think and want to say than on what our opponents will say and think. And we do not focus on achieving one important goal at a time working together. In 1997, child advocates stood for healthy children in over 700 local events in all fifty states. This focused witness coupled with a Cyber-Stand on the Internet and a broad-based coalition of over 100 national organizations co-convened by CDF and the American Cancer Society helped enact the bipartisan (Hatch-Kennedy) Child Health Insurance Program (CHIP). CHIP will provide $48 billion over the next ten years to provide free or affordable health coverage for five of the eleven million uninsured children. Most of these children live in working families whose employers do not provide health coverage. States have now got to implement CHIP effectively.

┦ LESSON 8: *Watch out for success. It can be more dangerous than failure.* "There is more to be learned in one day of discomfort, poverty, and anxiety than in a lifetime of apparent happiness, security, riches, and power," an anonymous sage said. Success tempts you to park on yesterday's and today's accomplishments and to relax vigilance. When you succeed you are often a target of those who cannot stand to see another get ahead. When you fail, you have to stop and figure out how to improve. A lot of America's current family and community breakdown and youth alienation may stem as much from too much material success as from poverty. Dr. Benjamin Mays said it plainly: "Cadillacs and Lincolns may keep you living but only your ideals will keep you alive. Youth is a time for dreaming great dreams and building air castles in great worlds. It is not how long you live but how well—always grasping—reaching forward. To be satisfied is to die."

℞ LESSON 9: *You can't do everything by yourself but you can do a lot.* Don't be a lone ranger who fails to reach out to and learn from others and try to reinvent every old wheel again. But don't think you have to wait until everybody agrees with you or comes along before you try to make a difference. Most people are never going to come along. I love to remember the three-thousand-year-old story of how three women —a mother, a sister, and a pharaoh's daughter—transcended caste, faith, and race to save one boy baby named Moses who became God's instrument to save the Hebrew people. I also love the story of the two slave midwives, Shiprah and Puah, who shrewdly disobeyed the pharaoh's order to kill all male Hebrew babies because they feared God more than the earthly king. These five very unlikely social revolutionaries are models for what a few individuals with commitment can do. My friend Rev. Otis Moss told a Haley Farm retreat group, "In your time, in your space, by God's grace, you can make a difference." In our time, working together, we can make an even bigger difference, by God's grace, for our children.

℞ LESSON 10: *Asking the right questions and measuring the right things may be more important than finding the right answers.* Many people confuse standardized test results with innate ability, leadership, and motivation. Dr. Charles Adams, Pastor of Detroit's Hartford Memorial Baptist Church, pointed out that neither Martin Luther King, Jr., nor Thomas Edison would have measured up on standardized tests, but one lit up the world through the light bulb and the other lit up the world through moral uplift. CDF's board chair and

Philadelphia school superintendent, David Hornbeck, who believes and is showing that all Philadelphia's children can achieve, says, "We get what we measure and we often measure the wrong thing." And Robert F. Kennedy eloquently reminded us in a University of Kansas speech that "Our gross national product . . . if we should judge America by that . . . does not allow for the health of our children, the quality of their education, or the joy of their play. It does not include the beauty of our poetry or the strength of our marriages; nor the intelligence of our public debate or the integrity of our public officials. It measures neither our wit nor our courage, neither our wisdom nor learning, neither our compassion nor devotion to our country. It measures everything in short, except that which makes life worthwhile. It can tell us everything about America except why we are proud that we are Americans."

‡ LESSON 11: *Travel lightly through life and resist the tyranny of burdensome or unneeded things.* More is not necessarily better. Tolstoy said that "he has much who needs least." King Saul gave the shepherd boy David heavy armor to go out to slay Goliath but the boy knew he would be unable to move or fight with it, relying instead on his strategic skill, slingshot, and God's grace. I am so burdened by taking care of all the things I have let myself be convinced I need in bouts of shopoholism. The more paper I throw out the more seems to pile up. I have more magazines than I can read, more newspapers than are worth reading, and more machines than I can usefully use that keep breaking down.

‡ LESSON 12: *Be a pilgrim and not a tourist in life and don't confuse heroism with fame or celebrity.* Cleveland, Ohio's Rev. Otis Moss says: "Pilgrims seek insights; tourists just want to see the sights." God has placed endless miracles and opportunities before us. See and hear them and be grateful. Learn the difference between heroism and celebrity and not to confuse money with meaning, educational degrees with wisdom and common sense, or power with worthwhile purpose. Someone has said, "The hero is known for achievements, the celebrity for being well known. Celebrities make the news, heroes make history. Time makes heroes, time dissolves celebrities."

୬ *LESSON 13: God has a job for all of us to do. Open up the envelope of your soul and try to discern the Creator's orders inside.* The Dan-
ish philosopher Søren Kierkegaard wrote that each of us comes to
earth with sealed orders from God. Struggle to find your orders and to
carry them out. Nobody can do it for you. Mrs. Mae Bertha Carter
echoed Kierkegaard's belief when asked a few weeks before she died
why she had been willing to risk violence and harassment to get her
children a good education. "It was in us to do it. You know, somebody
got to do it. We are born for a purpose. Everybody is born for a purpose. You were born for a good purpose. God has a job for all of us to
do." Seek your job and try to do it well.

୬ *LESSON 14: Follow the Golden Rule rather than the world's silver, iron, bronze, and copper rules.* Every great faith affirms the Golden
Rule, "Do unto others as you would have them do unto you," as the
key to peace and salvation. But my wonderful late friend and great
preacher, Dr. Samuel DeWitt Proctor, described how humankind has
downgraded it into four lesser ones to fit and justify rather than ele-
vate our conduct: *the silver rule*, do unto others as they have already
done unto you; *the iron rule*, do unto others as you fully expect them
to do unto you; *the bronze rule*, do unto others before they do unto
you; and *the copper rule*, do unto others and cut out.

୬ *LESSON 15: Bear all or most of the criticism and share all of the
credit.* Don't hog the limelight if you want to hold coalitions together
and keep friends. Daddy used to tell my mother, sister, brothers, and
me to step back and let others shine. If anybody in our congregation
could do a task at all, however less well than we could, he would always
say step back. I did not have a media or public relations staff person
during the first decade of CDF's existence. We were eager to get other
people adopting our words and vision as theirs. You can go a long way
in life if you do the work and give other people the credit.

୬ *LESSON 16: Be real. Try to do what you say, say what you
mean, and be what you seem.* Speak plainly and truthfully in this era in
which words are often used to manipulate rather than illuminate, to
hide rather than reveal the truth, to make big profit rather than good
policy, to make us forget rather than learn and listen, to comfort us
when we need to be challenged and to change, to help us avoid our-

selves and our problems rather than confront and struggle to solve them. Phoniness and calculated performances have become the norm in too much of our political and religious life. Too many preachers' sermons are attempts to stir up the congregational audience rather than expressions of reverence and gratitude to God. Soundbites for television have replaced complex truth, and filth and profanity are perceived as funny and acceptable language for children as four-letter words have proliferated in our culture. Try not to pretend to be what you are not. There is so much falsehood and pretension in politics, in business, in religion, and in the media that children feel unable to trust and believe anyone or anything. This breeds cynicism and despair. How sad it is that we have to tell our children that we don't want them to grow up to be like many of the people in power all around them.

⯈ LESSON 17: *Avoid high-maintenance, low-impact people and life in the fast lane.* Life's too short and precious to fritter it away on people who are more concerned about themselves than about helping others or serving a cause bigger than themselves. My brother Harry bought a 1935 Ford and fixed it up when he was in divinity school. He recounts how the old Ford did just fine going to and from Rochester, New York and Bennettsville, South Carolina until he decided to switch to the fast lane where it would shake violently and struggle to keep up as the faster cars zoomed by. Drugs and booze and guns and partying and sex may entice you out of the steady slower lane but they can wreck your life. Pull over to the side, think about your destination, and then travel there at a safe speed for yourself and others.

⯈ LESSON 18: *God did not create two classes of children or human beings—only one.* Never defer to another on the basis of color, income, gender, money, or title. Any adult who teaches Black, Brown, and White children that God our Creator values them unequally is not a hero but a heretic. I remember as a child hearing South Carolina's Senator James Byrnes, much esteemed in some circles, utter disparaging words of "never" which fell on my ears and pierced my heart as he urged fellow White citizens to resist *Brown* if the Supreme Court gave me a right to go to nondiscriminatory schools.

℘ LESSON 19: *Don't ever give up on life. It is God's gift. When trouble comes, hang in.* The old folks in my childhood always said God never closes one door without opening another. I believe this. I have watched with profound admiration a dear, wealthy young friend live so fully after learning he was infected with the AIDS virus. I first met him as a teenager. The decade after he learned he had HIV has been a truly remarkable and inspiring story of human courage and resiliency. He lives, as we all should, as if every day is his last and best, fully, joy-filled with singing, hiking, swimming, meditating, playing tennis, cooking, and working as a manager in his company. What a blessing he has bestowed on all who know and love him with his message that life is here and now and good and I will rejoice and be glad in it. I hope all those infected with HIV and any whose family members view it as a death rather than life sentence will take heart. While the new drug cocktails have not cured AIDS, they have shifted the debate to the quality of life with HIV for those able to afford them and are blessed with good health coverage. That's progress. I pray all those similarly affected by serious problems will transform them into life sentences.

℘ LESSON 20: *Strive hard to be a good parent.* It is as or more important than your career. This is true for fathers and mothers. "The biggest business in any society in any period is the nurturing, rearing, and cultivating of children," my father believed. Daddy laid out four key things parents ought to have or do: (1) a wide understanding and a deep appreciation of both your world and your children; (2) firm convictions; (3) the strength to give sensible counsel, positive discipline, and moral and spiritual poise in an age of strange irony; and (4) a commitment to, at all costs, maintain a home, a center of love for children's nurture and security.

℘ LESSON 21: *Be a good ancestor. Stand for something bigger than yourself. Add value to the Earth during your sojourn.* Give something back. Every minute you drink from wells you did not dig, are sheltered by builders you will never know, are protected by police and soldiers and neighbors and caretakers whose names are in no record books, are tended by healing hands of every hue and heritage, and are fed and clothed by the labors of countless others. Olive Schreiner, the

South African writer, said: "Where I lie down worn out, other men will stay young and fresh. By the steps I have cut they will climb; by the stairs that I have built they will mount. They may never know the name of the man (or woman) who made them. At the clumsy work they will laugh; when the stones roll they will curse me. But they will mount, and on my work, they will climb, and by my stair . . . And no man liveth to himself, and no man dies to himself." What will your obituary say? What will your legacy in life be?

╠○   LESSON 22: *Don't let anything or anybody get between you and your education.* This was my daddy's last word of advice to me as he lay dying in an ambulance as we were riding to the hospital. Mrs. Mae Bertha Carter, in an interview shortly before she died, recounted why she and her husband Matthew chopped and picked cotton and later endured violence, eviction, joblessness, and constant fear about their children's safety, mistreatment, ridicule, and isolation by White teachers and children: "Don't care where you go in this world, you need an education, so we stay on the farm, grow our food, send our children to school, and let them get an education. My basic message when I talk to children is to get an education, because without an education you nowhere."

╠○   LESSON 23: *Never judge the contents of a box by its wrappings.* Open it up before you buy or throw it out. This nation throws away billions of dollars and countless wealth in human potential by judging children and others by their extrinsic characteristics of color, gender, or background rather than by their intrinsic qualities and abilities. And don't get infatuated by or taken in by titles and position. Look beyond appearances to see if there is any substance or character behind them.

╠○   LESSON 24: *Take responsibility for your behavior. Don't make excuses, blame, or point fingers at others or hide behind "everybody's doing it."* So many urgent needs go unaddressed because we waste so much time and energy pointing fingers at someone else and doing nothing. Epidemic poverty, violence, and immorality in our society is the convergent cumulation of many factors. Pick one to tackle and do your part. So much selfish and destructive behavior is condoned because "everybody's doing it." Stop it with you.

❧ *LESSON 25: Possessions and power don't make the man or woman: principles, character, and love do.* "Man shall not live by bread alone, but by every word that proceedeth out of the mouth of God," St. Matthew reminded. Stocks and bonds, pearls and furs, money, houses, and land may be fun to have, and food and shelter are necessary to exist, but they do not add up to a life or lasting legacy. Material possessions have never made a person great if they are hoarded rather than shared to lift the lives of others. Nobody asks about Martin Luther King, Jr.'s possessions or remembers Robert Kennedy primarily because of his family's wealth; it was their growth into service for the poor and those left behind that we remember. "For those who want to save their life will lose it, and those who lose their life for my sake will save it." I hope the young people of today will lose the world, find themselves, and save America's soul.

☙ A GLOSSARY OF MENTORS ❧
AND SIGNIFICANT
OTHERS

This book shows how many significant adults influenced me at different stages in my life. I have profiled some of those who had the most profound impact but mention others who inspired and helped me grow throughout my life. I want young people to know about them. Like those I profile, they shared common characteristics of personal integrity, courage, persistence in the face of adversity, and a willingness to stand up against social injustice.

MARIAN ANDERSON, great Black contralto after whom I was named. Denied the right to perform at Washington, D.C.'s Constitution Hall by the Daughters of the American Revolution in 1939 because of her race, she sang before 75,000 people at the Lincoln Memorial with the help of Eleanor Roosevelt.

ELLA BAKER, the key catalyst behind the organizing of the SNCC— the Student Nonviolent Coordinating Committee. She also helped Dr. King's Southern Christian Leadership Conference understand the importance of infrastructure to movement building. Joanne Grant's biography, *Ella Baker: Freedom Bound*, gives an account of her life.

MARY MCLEOD BETHUNE, leading Black educator and women's leader and founder of Bethune-Cookman College and of the National Council of Negro Women.

UNITA BLACKWELL, a civil rights leader and former sharecropper who became the first Black woman mayor in Mississippi. A former MacArthur Prize Fellow, she is now serving a second stint as mayor of Mayersville, Mississippi.

AMIE BYERS, a stalwart member of Shiloh Baptist Church whom my mother sent to help me and my husband raise our three sons. She lived with our family for fourteen years.

MAE BERTHA CARTER, the first school desegregation plaintiff in Sunflower County, Mississippi and the first Black parent to exercise her "freedom of choice" to enroll eight of her children in previously all-White schools in Drew. The treatment of her children led her to court, where her challenge ended Mississippi's "freedom of choice," designed to prevent rather than enable Black children to get an equal education. Constance Curry's *Silver Rights* describes her struggles.

SEPTIMA CLARK, a Black South Carolina schoolteacher who won the right to equal pay for Black teachers in that state and headed the Citizenship Education Program at Highlander Folk Center near Knoxville, Tennessee and later for Martin Luther King, Jr.'s Southern Christian Leadership Conference.

WILLIAM SLOANE COFFIN, JR., former chaplain of Yale University, senior minister of Riverside Church in New York City, and head of SANE, a national organization seeking to stop the proliferation and use of nuclear weapons. His autobiography is *Once to Every Man*. He is also author of *A Passion for the Possible: A Message for U.S. Churches*.

SAMUEL DuBOIS COOK, a Morehouse College graduate and disciple of Dr. Benjamin E. Mays. A gifted professor of political science at Atlanta University who later became president of Dillard University in New Orleans, his political theory course greatly influenced me as a Spelman student.

OLIVE WRIGHT COVINGTON, my big sister, a graduate of Fisk University, was a teacher and teacher trainer in the public schools of the District of Columbia and of South Carolina. She directs CDF's office in Bennettsville which serves as the curriculum development laboratory for over forty CDF-sponsored Freedom Schools across the United States.

FREDERICK DOUGLASS, former slave and great abolitionist leader and orator. His autobiography, *Narrative of the Life of Frederick Douglass, an American Slave, Written by Himself*, chronicles his great life.

MEDGAR EVERS, head of the Mississippi National Association for the Advancement of Colored People (NAACP). Assassinated in 1963 by Byron de la Beckwith, who was finally convicted in 1998 thanks to the persistence of Medgar's widow, Myrlie. Medgar picked me up at the airport on my first trip to Mississippi. Myrlie Evers' book *For Us, the Living* is a record of their struggles.

FANNIE LOU HAMER, a key voice in and the soul of the Mississippi movement. She was a sharecropper who insisted on and sacrificed everything to achieve the right to vote. Kay Mills' *This Little Light of Mine* recounts her life.

AARON HENRY, president of the Mississippi NAACP, a pharmacist and civil rights leader in Clarksdale, Mississippi.

M. CARL HOLMAN, poet, journalist, and professor at Clark College who strongly supported the student movement in Atlanta. He later became deputy director of the U.S. Civil Rights Commission and succeeded John Gardner as head of the National Urban Coalition.

CHARLES HOUSTON, the brilliant conceptualizer and leader of a legal team including Thurgood Marshall, William Hastle, and James Nabrit, whose systematic legal strategy led to an end to public school segregation in *Brown v. Board of Education*. Genna Rae McNeil examines his extraordinary leadership in *Groundwork: Charles Hamilton Houston and the Struggle for Civil Rights*.

MORDECAI JOHNSON, first Black president of Howard University and contemporary of Dr. Benjamin E. Mays. I heard him speak several times as a child.

THERESA KELLY, a community elder in Bennettsville with whom I stayed when my parents went away. Our family had dinner with her on Sunday evenings.

ROBERT F. KENNEDY, former attorney general, Democratic senator from New York, and candidate for the Democratic presidential nomination when assassinated in June 1968. On a trip to Mississippi with a Senate subcommittee examining poverty programs he went with me to the Mississippi Delta to see poor families. He became a passionate advocate to end hunger and poverty, and suggested a Poor People's Campaign which Dr. King began planning before his death.

MARTIN LUTHER KING, JR., principal leader of the Montgomery Civil Rights Movement and moral voice of the national Civil Rights Movement. His "I Have a Dream" speech at the Lincoln Memorial, witness against the Vietnam War, and call for a Poor People's Campaign made him America's leading prophet and practitioner of nonviolent direct action in the twentieth century.

LUCY MCQUEEN, a community elder and Sunday school teacher in whose Bennettsville home I sometimes stayed.

MALCOLM X, fiery, charismatic Black Muslim leader who was assassinated in 1965. He overcame early and difficult obstacles of racism and turned away from criminal activity to become a major Black American leader. With Alex Haley's assistance, his extraordinary life was chronicled in *The Autobiography of Malcolm X*.

JOHN DAVID MAGUIRE, a Freedom Rider with Yale chaplain Bill Coffin, fellow Wesleyan University professor David Swift, and Yale law student George Smith. He later became president of the State University of New York at Old Westbury and of Claremont Graduate University.

THURGOOD MARSHALL, first Black justice of the United States Supreme Court and solicitor general of the United States. He headed the NAACP Legal Defense Fund and Educational Fund and was the lead attorney in *Brown v. Board of Education* which outlawed public school segregation in 1954.

BENJAMIN ELIJAH MAYS, president of Morehouse College between 1940 and 1967 and a mentor of many of my mentors including Dr. Martin Luther King, Jr., Dr. Otis Moss, and Dr. Samuel DuBois Cook. He chaired the Atlanta school board after retiring from Morehouse's presidency. His autobiography is *Born to Rebel*.

CHARLES E. MERRILL, JR., educator, founder, and headmaster for many years at the Commonwealth School in Boston. He chaired the Morehouse board of trustees for over a decade and created fellowships which enabled Morehouse and Spelman students and faculty to study and travel abroad. I spent fifteen months in Europe during my junior year at Spelman College on a Merrill Fellowship.

AMZIE MOORE, a pillar of the Civil Rights Movement in Cleveland, Mississippi who shepherded me and other young civil rights workers through the ropes of survival.

BOB MOSES, now director of the Algebra Project and a former MacArthur Prize Fellow, initiated in 1961 the Mississippi voter registration organizing campaign for the Student Nonviolent Coordinating Committee (SNCC). His remarkable leadership in the Mississippi movement is chronicled in Taylor Branch's *Pillar of Fire: America in the King Years 1963–1965.*

OTIS MOSS, pastor of the Olivet Institutional Baptist Church in Cleveland, Ohio, civil rights activist who succeeded Dr. Martin Luther King, Jr., as co-pastor with Dr. Martin Luther King, Sr., of Ebenezer Baptist Church in Atlanta, Georgia. Key voice in the Atlanta Civil Rights Movement, he currently chairs Morehouse College's board of trustees, CDF's Black Church Initiative, and is worship leader of the annual Samuel DeWitt Proctor Institute for Child Advocacy Ministry at CDF–Haley Farm.

ROSA PARKS, catalyst for the Montgomery bus boycott and the launching of the Civil Rights Movement. She heads the Raymond and Rosa L. Parks Institute and is the author of *Rosa Parks: My Story* and *Quiet Strength.*

SAMUEL DEWITT PROCTOR, great preacher and educator. President of A&T and Virginia Union Universities and successor to Adam Clayton Powell, Jr., as senior minister at Abyssinian Baptist Church in New York City. He was first worship leader of the Institute for Child Advocacy Ministry at Haley Farm, now named for him. In *My Moral Odyssey* he describes the development of his moral consciousness.

LILLIAN SMITH, white southern writer and fighter for racial and gender equality. Her books include *Strange Fruit* and *Killers of the Dream.*

HOWARD THURMAN, influential Black theologian who was the first dean of the chapel at Howard University, co-founder of the Fellowship of All Peoples in San Francisco, and dean of the chapel at Boston University. I was privileged to hear this prolific writer and eloquent speaker in chapel at Spelman College.

SOJOURNER TRUTH, former slave woman and eloquent voice for the abolition of slavery and equal rights for Blacks and women. Her life is chronicled in Nell Painter's *Sojourner Truth: A Life, A Symbol.*

HARRIET TUBMAN, fearless former slave who shepherded other slaves to freedom on her daring underground railroad. She is often referred to as the Black Moses.

WATIES WARING, courageous federal district judge from South Carolina who was considered a traitor by Whites who opposed his decisions outlawing the Whites-only primary and equalizing compensation for White and Black teachers in South Carolina.

BOOKER T. WASHINGTON, the extraordinary Black educator and leader. Born a slave, he taught at Hampton Institute from which he graduated and served as president of Tuskegee Institute. His influential autobiography *Up from Slavery* recounts his life. He was the most powerful Black leader of his time rivalled only by W. E. B. DuBois.

KATE WINSTON, a warm, kind church woman who visited my hometown in the summers and spoiled me with fancy clothes and attention.

ARTHUR JEROME WRIGHT, SR., my father and role model who served as pastor of the Shiloh Baptist Church in Bennettsville, South Carolina for twenty-five years. At Shiloh, he succeeded Dr. J. J. Starks, the first Black president of Benedict College in Columbia, South Carolina, who was his mentor.

HARRY STARKS WRIGHT, SR., my brother and surrogate father after Daddy died. A Morehouse graduate, he left Colgate-Rochester Divinity School to assume our father's responsibilities as pastor of Shiloh Baptist Church. He later earned his doctorate of divinity at Southern Methodist University and served as chaplain and president of Bishop College.

MAGGIE LEOLA BOWEN WRIGHT, my mother, who served as church organist, choir director, principal fundraiser, organizer of the Mothers' Club, and general partner in my father's ministry at Shiloh. She carried on these tasks for thirty years after his death.

ANDREW YOUNG, Dr. King's chief lieutenant at the Southern Christian Leadership Conference who became the first Black congressman from Georgia since Reconstruction. He later served as U.S. ambassador to the United Nations during the Carter Administration and as mayor of Atlanta. His autobiography is *Way Out of No Way: The Spiritual Memoirs of Andrew Young* and he is author of *Easy Burden: The Civil Rights Movement and the Transformation of America.*

JACK YOUNG, R. JESS BROWN, AND CARSIE HALL, the only Black civil rights attorneys when I moved to Mississippi who provided me guidance, support, and legal cover until I could gain admission to the Mississippi Bar. They represent the extraordinarily brave band of lawyers throughout the South whose behind-the-scenes legal support enabled the Civil Rights Movement to succeed.

VIVIAN YOUNG, friend and civil leader who befriended me during my junior year abroad in Geneva, Switzerland, where her husband Joe worked for the International Labor Organization (ILO). She now heads Stand for Children in Delaware.

HOWARD ZINN, chair of the history department at Spelman College when I was a student and later a Boston University faculty member. A prolific writer, his books include *The Southern Mystique, SNCC: The New Abolitionists, A People's History of the United States, Declarations of Independence,* and *You Can't Be Neutral on a Moving Train.*

❦ WORKS CITED ❧

Barboza, Steven, ed. *The African American Book of Values* (Double-day, 1998).

Blackwell, Unita. Taped interview with the Children's Defense Fund at the former Alex Haley Farm, CDF's center for spiritual renewal and leadership development.

Branch, Taylor. *Parting the Waters: America in the King Years 1954–1963* (Simon and Schuster, 1998), *Pillar of Fire: America in the King Years 1963–1965* (Touchstone, 1999). Tape of speech at Children's Defense Fund forum at the Civil Rights Museum, Memphis, Tenn.

Carter, Mae Bertha. Taped interviews with Children's Defense Fund at Haley Farm and in her home in Drew, Miss., 1999.

Children's Defense Fund. *A Chronology of the Children's Defense Fund* (CDF, 1998).

Clark, Septima. *Ready from Within.* Edited by Cynthia Stokes Brown (African World Press, Inc., 1990).

Coles, Dr. Robert. *The Story of Ruby Bridges* (Scholastic, 1995).

Curry, Constance. *Silver Rights* (Algonquin, 1995).

Gates, Henry Louis, Jr., and Nellie Y. McKay, eds. *The Norton Anthology of African American Literature* (W. W. Norton, 1996).

Gide, André. *The Immoralist*. Translated by Stanley Applebaum (Dover, 1996).

Grant, Joanne. *Ella Baker: Freedom Bound* (John Wiley & Sons, 1998).

Henderson, Michael. *The Forgiveness Factor* (Grosvenor Books, 1996).

Holy Bible.

Homer. *The Odyssey*, tr. by W. H. D. Rouse (Mentor, 1937), and tr. by Robert Fagles (Penguin, 1999).

Horton, Myles, with Herbert and Judith Kohl, contributors. *The Long Haul: An Autobiography* (Doubleday, 1990).

Kennedy, Robert F. Speeches obtained from John F. Kennedy Library, Boston, Mass.

Lanker, Brian. *I Dream a World: Portraits of Black Women Who Changed America* (Stewart, Tabori & Chang, 1989).

Lerner, Gerda, ed. *Black Women in White America* (Vintage, 1972).

Malcolm X. *The Autobiography of Malcolm X* (Ballantine, 1964).

Marsh, Charles. *God's Long Summer: Stories of Faith and Civil Rights* (Princeton Univ. Press, 1958).

Mays, Benjamin E. *Quotable Quotes* (Vintage, 1983).

Mills, Kay. *This Little Light of Mine: The Life of Fannie Lou Hamer* (Plume, 1994).

National Conference of Catholic Bishops. "Putting Children and Families First: A Challenge for Our Church, Nation, and the World," a pastoral letter, 1991.

Outward Bound. *Readings from the Hurricane Island Outward Bound School* (Rockland, Maine).

Proctor, Dr. Samuel DeWitt. Tape of sermon at CDF's Institute for Child Advocacy Ministry held at the Alex Haley Farm.

Quinn, Tracey, ed. *Quotable Women of the Twentieth Century* (Bill Adler Books, Inc., 1999).

Smith, Lillian. *How Am I To Be Heard: Letters of Lillian Smith*. Edited by Margaret Rose Gladney (Univ. of North Carolina Press, 1996).

The Talmud.

Taylor, Dr. Gardner. Tape of sermon at CDF's Institute for Child Advocacy Ministry held at the Alex Haley Farm.

Thurman, Howard. *Deep Is the Hunger* (Harper, 1951), *The Growing Edge* (Friends United Press, 1974), *Jesus and the Disinherited* (Beacon Press, 1996).

Tolstoy, Leo. *A Calendar of Wisdom*. Translated by Peter Sekirin (Scribner, 1997).

Washington, James Melvin, ed. *A Testament of Hope: The Essential Writings and Speeches of Martin Luther King, Jr.* (Harper, 1991).

Young, Andrew. Tape of the Children's Defense Fund forum at the Civil Rights Museum, Memphis, Tenn., and tape of the CDF meeting at the Alex Haley Farm.

Zinn, Howard. *Declarations of Independence* (HarperCollins, 1990), *SNCC: The New Abolitionists* (Greenwood, 1985).

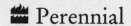 Perennial

Books by Marian W. Edelman:

LANTERNS
A Memoir of Mentors
ISBN 0-06-095859-6 (paperback)

When a young Edelman expressed dismay at receiving punishment for a slight infraction, her teacher told her, "To whom much is given, much is expected." Such messages are the heart of this book. Marian Wright Edelman shares stories from her life at the center of this century's most dramatic civil rights and child advocacy struggles, and pays tribute to those great men and women who lit her way.

"[Edelman's] arms are open to the children and adults of the world and we all are stronger and more safe because of her." —Maya Angelou

GUIDE MY FEET
Prayers and Meditations for Our Children
ISBN 0-06-095819-7 (paperback)

Prayers and meditations for parents and others who strive to instill values of faith, integrity, and service in our children at a time when these ideals are threatened by commercialism and violence.

"Marian Edelman blends gospel passages with her own personal prayers and her reverence for the young brings a depth to this book that goes well beyond the words." —Los Angeles Times

THE MEASURE OF OUR SUCCESS
Letters to My Children and Yours
ISBN 0-06-097546-6 (paperback)

The Measure of Our Success carries a compassionate message for parents trying to raise moral children. Edelman has written a tough and searching book that ought to be required reading for every American, especially parents and young people.

"This book is filled with wisdom and inspiration. I recommend it to everyone concerned about the future of our children." —Bill Cosby

Available wherever books are sold, or call 1-800-331-3761 to order.